How to be a Wedding Planner

Barbara Collins

AuthorHouse™ UK Ltd.
500 Avebury Boulevard
Central Milton Keynes, MK9 2BE
www.authorhouse.co.uk
Phone: 08001974150

First published by AuthorHouse 5/11/2010

ISBN: 978-1-4490-8121-8 (sc)

Photographs on cover courtesy of Alison and Steve Forrest, Elmcroft Studios www.elmcroftstudios.com

This book is printed on acid-free paper.

authorHOUSE®

Contents

Foreword

I founded Every Detail, a Wedding Planning and Consultancy company in 2001, and took it from an idea in my mind to a leading franchised wedding planning business, through to selling the company in 2009.

From the company's early days in 2001, through to today, I have learnt so many valuable lessons which I share with you in this insightful book. Whilst writing this manual, I have been open and honest as I want you to have the very best start in your career as a wedding planner, and hopefully when you reach the end of this book you can 'hit the ground' running.

I am often asked to comment on the Wedding Planning industry – both in the press and on the television. In 2005, I made a documentary for Discovery Home and Health which followed the planning of two weddings through to the wedding days. In addition, I've been Champney's resident wedding expert and the National Wedding Show's 'Inspiration Zone' Speaker in 2008. I now work internationally training aspiring wedding planners, assist small businesses and work with prestigious hotels and wedding venues to improve their wedding services.

So, get reading and very good luck, I wish you all the very best in and a prosperous and enjoyable wedding planning career.

Barbara Collins
Director
The Wedding Training Company Limited.

Role of the Wedding Planner

Welcome to the world of weddings and the very demanding role of the wedding planner!

There are many different job titles for a wedding planner that you will often hear:- Wedding Co-ordinator, Wedding Advisor, Wedding Consultant, Wedding Designer, Wedding Organiser and Wedding Planner. With the exception of wedding co-ordinators, you could argue that the job titles are all the same role. There are some exceptions and these are open to interpretation.

Typically a wedding planner has general skills, (therefore not focused on one role or special area of the wedding plans) and can be the first point of call for the bridal couple on any aspect of their day. They are with the Bride and Groom from the moment they are hired to choreograph the wedding from beginning to end.

Wedding Planners, Organisers and Arrangers could all be the same role. They will work on behalf of their client, almost always independently of any particular supplier to ensure that the most suitable suppliers are recommended, chosen and booked, and not those that they have a financial interest in.

> Therefore a wedding planner needs to be:
>
> Well rounded with a variety of skills
> Comfortable at being the first point of call
> Able to get on well with all people
> Able to solve problems quickly and sensibly
> Full of ideas – inspirational, affordable, creative and realistic
> Able to keep track of expenditure
> Comfortable with running their own small business
> Able to manage relationships with Supplier and Clients
> Up to date with wedding trend and fashion

In essence, a successful wedding planner needs to be able to do what they have said they will do.

It is a common statement by wedding planners that they can get discounts and save brides and grooms significant money. If the planner has promised to get discounts on suppliers' prices through their contacts or excellent negotiation skills, then they should be able to do that, and be confident that they can. Likewise, if they have sold their brilliant design and theme ideas then those clients who book will want to feel very quickly that they can come up with and show imaginative, leading and very impressive ideas that they can tell all their friends and families about in years to come.

Independent wedding planners need to be prepared to work very hard, long hours and with little financial reward in the early days. Learning any new job takes time, and being a successful independent wedding planner will also take time. Be easy on yourself if you make mistakes, it's all part of the learning process.

A Wedding Consultant, tends to be some one who is well known and respected in the industry and writes articles, gives professional advice (in magazines/tv), and may present at wedding shows and train people through running training courses or providing advice and guidance to wedding venues to help improve their wedding offerings and increase their sales.

Wedding Designers, can be wedding planners that specialise in creating a truly amazing theme and look for a wedding day. They almost always also 'plan' the wedding too, but their main selling point is their ability to design a memorable wedding.

Wedding Co-ordinators are people who assist in the organisation of the wedding day, but do not make the main arrangements themselves. Typically they will either work for a wedding venue, or be hired by the Bride and Groom to be there on the day as an independent person and oversee the plans that have been made.

A Wedding Co-ordinator who works independently from a venue tends to offer what is known as an 'On the Day' Service, this is being involved with the couple in the lead up to their wedding day. The main duty is to work with the Bride and Groom in the preceding weeks to understand their day, the decisions that they've made and the suppliers they've chosen.

The 'On the Day' service is a flexible service that will suit every wedding regardless of venue. The service offers an experienced wedding co-ordinator who will be there from the morning of the wedding to oversee the lay up, put out favours, name cards, etc. The co-ordinator will be expected to be at the marriage venue to support the wedding party and then go on to the reception to be there when guests arrive, ensure all suppliers have set up, or made deliveries as per the arrangements and that everything proceeds to plan. Wedding Day Co-ordinators tend to stay all day and go home at a time they think is suitable, some stay until the first dance and others leave earlier at the speeches.

A Venue Co-ordinator works with the couple but tends to concentrate on the items and information that the venue needs to know, such as numbers, menu choice, arrival time and to oversee the contractual arrangements with the couple.

The wedding couple come to rely on the wedding co-ordinator because it's their point of contact, but are normally very disappointed that the person isn't there and attending their wedding on their wedding day. This has led to the need and popularity of the independent wedding co-ordinator.

To be a wedding planner you will need to be able to have good relationships with both clients and suppliers. Your clients should want to work with you when they meet you. If you are open about who you are and how you work, you should attract clients who like your style and the services that you offer. It is advisable that you begin to think now about the kind of person you are, why you will be a good wedding planner – what are your strengths and what are your weaknesses.

It is important to have considered this so that you can sell your strengths and concentrate those attributes to the key aspects of your business, but equally allow yourself the time to discover and correct your weaknesses.

Complete the table and detail your own strengths and weaknesses, this information will be helpful to you later on when you begin to think about your business plan and design of your business and discover:

WHAT KIND OF WEDDING PLANNER ARE YOU?

Strengths	Weaknesses
Example: "I am really good at being able to think of ideas – especially in tricky situations"	Example: "I am not very good at accounting and book keeping"

Once you've considered your strengths and weaknesses – it is time to start thinking about <u>why</u> you want to be a wedding planner.

Why I want to be a wedding planner

What I think will be the best part of the job

What I think will be the worst part of the job

Why will I be a good wedding planner

Starting your business 2

2.1 GET ADVICE

There are many places to turn to for advice on how to set up a small business. It is important to get independent advice on how to set up and run a business. In the UK there are organisations that have been set up to help small businesses start, develop and progress their businesses. There are free seminars and websites offering templates and advice. They also offer one to one advice and will hold networking events to help you meet similar businesses. In most countries, this advice and support is available and is worth seeking out and utilising.

Launching a new business is not easy, and success is not always guaranteed. Businesses are most likely to fail during the early years of trading, with 20 per cent of new businesses folding within their first year and 50 per cent within their first three years.

These figures should not scare you off, but should prepare you for some of the challenges you face when starting a business. With hard work and an awareness of the issues, your new business can be a great success.

Whilst we aren't going to go through all the mistakes that can be made and how to avoid them, we can help you focus on some of the important elements that you must do and also suggest how you can avoid making some of the most common mistakes.

It is important to take time to think about your business, what you want it to be and how you are going to operate it. For instance, will you run it on your own, or with a partner, will you look to expand and take on employees or freelance staff? You've already started the work by considering your strengths and weaknesses and the key skills you'll bring to the role, why you want to do it and what you want your business to be.

'Fail to plan - plan to fail'

It is important to start to think about the business' name, the logo, design, pricing, and where you will operate and what services you will offer.

You will have to consider the financial risk - will you need to keep up alternative employment at the start of your venture to provide you with guaranteed income? If you are working during the day, then you will need to think about how you'll feel to not have a social life - will you be able to not go out so much in the evenings because you'll be working so much? Will you have the confidence to meet new people all the time, which can sometimes be quite challenging, and will you have the drive to keep going when at times it can be really tough. You have to be very honest with yourself about your level of commitment. We will look into this more at the 'business plan' section.

2.2 MARKET RESEARCH

Research and planning are vital to ensure that your business starts off well and has a chance of longevity. A common misconception is that small businesses fail simply through lack of sufficient funding or did not put the right team in place. However, many fail because they have not spent enough time researching their business idea and its viability in the market. A good starting place is to see who your competition is, and what they offer. You don't need to style yourself on them – instead you should stay with what you think will work (again, based on you, who you are and your strengths, weaknesses and what you want your business to feel like and offer).

The best place to start your research is the wedding industry itself. Who are the local suppliers? What market do they aim for? What venues are there and are they the type of venues that will attract clients who will appreciate the role of a wedding planner? Widen your area and see if your findings are still the same, or does the target market and, therefore, the services offered change as you look at different villages, towns and cities.

All successful businesses need to have a close understanding of their potential and existing customers and the marketplace that they work in. With this knowledge you will be able to sell effectively, price competitively, compare yourself with other similar businesses and spot new opportunities. We have spoken considerably about who you are, and what you will offer. You will need to put these thoughts together with your research to ensure that what you are offering is wanted in the area you will market it.

Lack of proper market research is one of the key problems for new businesses. It's easy to get carried away with a business idea and set up a business without testing whether it will work. As tempting as it is to just 'go for it' when you have your idea clear in your mind, it really is recommended to sit down and seriously think about all the aspects of your business and not just 'planning people's weddings'.

You can get an idea of general trends - such as number of people marrying, number of first marriages/ remarriages, and their age groups from the National Statistics.

You can also carry out some field research. This data will help you to not be too optimistic about the number of wedding clients you may get with the first six months, year etc.

Think about some questions that you will want to ask in your research…how will you know that what you are thinking of proposing will be well received and is needed in the wedding market?

What do I want to ask?	Who is the best person to ask?
Example: Would you like to work with a wedding planner? Do you work with any already	Wedding Supplier
Example: What was the one thing on your wedding day you would do differently? Could having a wedding planner have changed this?	Recently married bride

SOME IDEAS FOR RESEARCH:

Try to contact the people you ultimately aim to sell to and try to find out:

- who your potential customers are and what groups they fall into?
- are there major employers in your area, and what kind of professionals do they employ?
- how much of your kind of product or service they already buy from your competitors
- how many would consider a wedding planner (and did they book or not – why not?)
- the criteria on which they make buying decisions (choice of service or price)
- what it would take to get them to buy from you
- how, when and where they prefer to buy

Once you have started to develop your ideas from your findings, talk about them! Failing to share your business ideas with people you trust means that you will miss out on objective feedback. Friends and family are good people to share your ideas with. Recently married or soon to be married friends and acquaintances are even better, as they are living and breathing weddings and will have the most up to date and real life view for you and will give you a valuable perspective.

Keep track of these ideas and suggestions so that you can use them in your business plan and they can help in developing your business' services. You could also devise a very short questionnaire and go to wedding shows and ask brides to be if they will give you their views.

By not doing your research, you are in danger of selling to the wrong people or of not understanding your marketplace, and subsequently wasting a lot of money on advertising and you won't get any bookings.

Spend some time here thinking of research you should undertake, and what it is you are looking to find out about to help you in this stage of your business planning and design.

Question	Where to look?
Example: *Types of wedding venues in the area*	Wedding websites, yellow pages, internet, Registry Office will have a list of all venues that are licensed to perform wedding ceremonies.
Example: *Target market the most popular wedding suppliers/ shops/ market*	Ask recently married couples which suppliers they chose, then go and meet the suppliers.
Example: *How popular are civil weddings compared to Church weddings*	Registry Office and local Parish Offices
Example: *Is there a desire for people who live away from the area to come here to be married?*	Registry Office will have information on the number of weddings recorded in the District

A decision you will need to make at some point (before you open a bank account!) is the type of business that you would want to have.

Sole Trader: This is a very popular business type for an independent Wedding Planner. It is the simplest way to run a business. Keeping records and accounts is straightforward, you need to account for your in goings and outgoings, but it means you get to keep all the profit. However, it also means that you are personally liable for all debts that your business incurs and if your business can not meet the payment, then you must do so from your own finances. You are also responsible for making sure that you pay all taxes and National Insurance contributions.

Partnership: A partnership is where two or more people will set up a business together. In a partnership, each partner is self-employed and takes a share of the profits, and they also share the risks, costs, and responsibilities of being in business. However, like being a sole trader, the partners are responsible for ensuring that all debts are paid, which means that they are personally liable to make the payments even if the business can not afford to do so.

Should you be considering setting up in partnership, you will need to ensure that you have considered the responsibilities that each of the partners will have, and the proportion of payment/salary each partner will receive. As the business does not exist in its own right (like a limited company) if one of the partners resigns, dies or goes bankrupt, the partnership must be dissolved but the business may not need to cease, you could re-establish it under a different business type. It is recommended that you take out a contract to establish the relationship between the partners, clearly lying out responsibilities, investment amounts and expectations of each partner.

Limited Company: There are varying types of limited companies and it is worth researching this first. Owning a limited company comes with more rules and regulations on how you display your address on your website and your stationery through to how you must file your accounts. However, limited companies exist in their own right. This means the company's finances are separated from the personal finances of their owners, and so should you need to dissolve the business due to lack of funds, the debts will stay with the company and not be the responsibility of the owners.

Deciding on this at the beginning will help you in the way that you structure your company. If you do decide to have a limited company then you will need to formally register the address at which the company is registered. Many formation companies or accountants will do this for you and submit the required paperwork to Companies House. You can easily do this yourself by following the information and advice on the Companies House website.

2.4 Name

There isn't a lot of advice that this book can give about choosing the name of your company, as ultimately this is your decision. We can, however, suggest that even though it seems along way off, you need to bear in mind your long term business goals. Do you want to be a multi-national company and if so will your name translate easily when you set up in France, Brazil or America for instance? Will you feel comfortable calling a Vicar, Registrar, Mother of the Bride and saying 'Hi, I am calling from 'Funky Wedding Planners"?

Ultimately, the choice of business name is your decision. During your research you are likely to come across many companies already in existence whose names you don't like, and many you do – and hopefully not the one that you really want. When choosing a name, check that the domain name is also available (www..... co.uk/com).

2.5 Business Plan

When you want to open your business bank account, you may find that the bank will ask to see your Business Plan. You will definitely be asked for your business plan if you want funding (such as a loan or grant).

Your business plan will become a close friend during your business start up days. Within it you'll be documenting your business ideas, your projected revenue, design and marketing ideas and also your approach to selling, pricing and wedding planning. The work that you have done so far will form part of the business plan.

Creating your business plan, may take more than a day. You do need to think about it carefully, as effectively it is a document that sets out what it is your business will do, and how it will operate. As you think about your business, it is worth making notes immediately as the thoughts come into your mind, and then go back and work on your business plan at a convenient time. There is a table for you to complete on the following page which lays out the key messages, you can record your ideas and thoughts here, and then refer back to it when you're writing your formal business plan.

The questions below are to help prompt your thinking and challenge your ideas so that they will help form the basis of any decisions you may take at a later date. You can keep coming back to this as you go through the manual and get more and more ideas.

Activity	
What do you intend to do? (i.e. Destination Weddings, Only 'on the day' services, an interactive website etc)	
What are your key selling points? (can you speak languages and be able to do 'destination weddings' or are you an expert sales person?)	
Do you have a 'vision' or 'mission statement'	
How are you going to develop the business?	
Who will be involved in the business start up and general management?	

What their skills are and their role? (above)	
Your estimated revenue? (What will you HAVE to make to break-even)	
How you will manage the budget?	
How will you accept payment?	
Will you use your home address? What phone number? (new mobile/landline…)	

The business plan should include an executive summary - this is an overview of the business you want to start. This is very important. The bank and other lenders/investors will make their initial decision about your business based on this section.

Keep it as honest as possible, and then you can refer back to it at times of despair if you need some motivation, or for direction if you are beginning to sway slightly from your original intentions.

The Executive Summary is a summary and therefore is usually written last. It details the main parts of all the other sections of the business plan, into a synopsis at the beginning of the document.

It should be no more than two pages long, interesting and informative. There are many templates available for free download on business plans, but to help you start now, you may want to consider writing it in these sections:

The Business Opportunity –This section describes your company vision. It also includes who you are and what your skills are, what you believe you have to offer and the market that you want to enter. This whole section will describe why your business is viable.

The Market – The market research that you have done, is detailed in this section, where you will give information on the market, who your competitors are and their position in the market place. You should also detail who your customers are and how you know that they will be interested in your product, and finally what the anticipated changes in the market place in the future will be, and how you anticipate your competitors will react. You should be looking to see that there is growth in that area (will big employers stay, are new executive homes being built, are the wedding venues popular and profitable?)

Marketing – Often the poorest section in a business plan, so do spend time on this area to really understand the specific activities that you intend to use to sell your business and its services. You should also consider in here how much you are willing to spend on marketing, how you will measure it's success, where will you target your advertising (in wedding magazines, the internet, at wedding shows?). It is advisable to set a budget for your annual advertising commitments.

The Team – This part of the plan outlines who will be involved in the business; their skills and the role that they will play. It is also worth including their financial commitment to the business and their availability to work on the business. Include any advisers that you have, such as solicitors and accountants and their charges. Also include any training or development you have planned. Don't feel that you have to have a big team around you to be a success. Many wedding planning companies are sole traders, and run by one person, but the key is to know when you need help, and the importance of that help (i.e. Do you need someone to proof read your documents now and again, or do you need an accountant or a graphic designer?)

Operations – This part of the plan details your operations, easier to fill out if you were a shop and therefore you could detail your stock control procedures etc. You can complete your office location, the type of equipment that you'll be using and where you suggest you meet your clients and suppliers. You can also enter here how you will price for your services, when you will ask for payment and how you will invoice etc.

Financial Forecasts – You will need to include your forecast revenue, i.e. what you imagine you will make in the first month, six months, year etc. You will also need to detail how you will repay money if you plan to borrow it, whether you'll be paying yourself a salary and what your daily running costs are. You can then remember these costs, when you get to pricing your services, and you must try to recoup as much of your overheads and running costs as possible.

Your Plan – You need to keep your plan professional looking, so ensure that it is well typed, spell checked and easy to read. Keep updating it, not only then will you have it on hand if needed, but also it will help keep you focused on achieving your long term goals and keeping on top of your business development.

You will also need to consider:

Money:	Where will you get the money to fund your business? Will you be investing any money? How will you earn your salary (do you need to?)
Legal Structure:	Partnership/Sole Trader/Limited Company?
Insurance:	What insurance will you need? Professional Indemnity Insurance and/or Public Liability insurance
Workplace:	Will you have an office? Where will you meet clients?
Taxes & Returns:	Do you know what to do and when? If not, speak to you local tax office or find an accountant.
Website & Promotion:	Get a well designed (and supported) website and company image

You will need to think about your need for business insurance, whether you'll need public liability, professional indemnity insurance and, if you are working from home, will you need to change your household insurance? It is worth comparing prices and checking what it is you really need, as you may not need both insurances if you are not having clients come to your premises.

Website and Literature. 3

As you are probably aware, the website is your biggest selling tool, in effect it is your shop window, and is where you should invest your money and time. If you don't have the skills yourself, do consider commissioning a graphic designer and web developer. They will help you to develop your branding and company image.

To help you to start to formulate your ideas, look through websites (for any service) and keep a note of the ones that you like and why. Likewise, do the same for adverts that you see whether they be online or in magazines.

By doing this you can start to get a clear idea in your mind of the style of your website, logos and general 'look and feel' of your business. Try to imagine the logo you have chosen being used on everything (car, clothes, leaflets, website etc).

Use the table below to record your likes and dislikes of other websites and advertising you see. Having a good look around will help you to begin to know what you like and what colours you see your business having. Once you have an idea of the colour schemes you like, and the styles of websites you like, you can share these ideas with your graphic designer and start to work on your own branding and designs.

Flick through magazines and cut out any you like, especially those that immediately catch your eye (whether you like them or not!). The following page is purposely left blank for you to attach ideas of adverts you like.

Websites I like:	Adverts I like:

Start to think about the messages that you want to convey on your website – they should link into your business plan, and describe what's different and great about you! Your website should contain enough information to provide the reader with a confidence that you are able to do the job, and that they would be interested in using you, but you may not want to give all of your information away on the website. It is recommended that you retain the finer details (such as pricing) for your brochures and stationery that you send to brides and grooms once they have made contact.

Each venue and supplier in the wedding industry has a different approach when it comes to their portfolio and demonstrating their expertise.

The way you choose to do it needs to be right for you

On your website and in any brochures you need to demonstrate your capability, make sure that you show your services at its best, try to take photographs with 'BEFORE' and 'AFTER' shots, to show how a room can be transformed, and the type of wedding you can 'create'. This will capture the Bride and Groom as they can then imagine their wedding and what you could do for them.

Courtesy of Every Detail Wedding Planners

Courtesy of Stephanie Mackrill
Photography
www.stephaniemackrill.com

The pictures of cakes shown here demonstrate how a picture can work and not work. The cake on the left, whilst very nice does not inspire brides nor sell you as someone who is associated with a professional, impressive and beautiful wedding. With photos in your brochure like this – you won't sell your services. However, with pictures (like that on the right) that look inviting and inspiring, your potential customers will more likely want to come and see you.

Testimonials are very valuable. Asking clients for feedback after you have worked with them will provide you with comments that you can use to showcase your service, and tell customers how previous clients have found your service. Some couples like to see testimonials from previous couples or will request to see references. You can consider putting a small selection of testimonials on your website. In the early days it can be hard to have these, so asking suppliers you have worked with to write a testimonial too can show that you are good to work with, a trustworthy and respected wedding planner.

Couples will look at their brochure of their chosen suppliers over and over again, so they need to be inspiring and 'classic' and explain your services well. They are likely to show their brochures and information to friends and family, and, therefore you should ensure that they are of a high quality to inspire and interest potential clients.

The key to successfully promoting your business and your brand is to be consistent.

Make sure that your website uses the *same colours* and *logo* as the rest of your marketing materials (e.g. letterhead, business cards, brochures, etc.). Having one look for your printed materials and another for your website will dilute your brand and confuse your customers. Likewise repeat the same messages in your stationery, keep your efforts focused and consistent, and your brand will be reinforced to your customers and help to establish you in the marketplace and support the professionalism of your business. There is competition in the wedding planning industry and a professional image will stand you in good stead against your competition. Websites are the most powerful tool and will be the place where the large majority of your potential customers will look at or hear about your company first.

Your website needs to be well designed, hosted well, and perform well (i.e. load quickly). The website also needs to be well written, each page should have a goal and a clear message. Do think about using music. Many customers may look at your site at work and won't want sound to just appear! If you do use sound, make sure you make it obvious where they can mute it!

Organise your pages sensibly; will your audience understand how to navigate it? They didn't write your site, and therefore don't know where you put each piece of information, so use descriptive links and write clearly. Try to avoid using pop up windows if you can, and choose the text colour that you use carefully, it should always be easy to read.

Having a stat-counter on display has little value, there isn't a reason for you to show on your site how many visitors you've had (unless you have a genuinely good reason then go for it). If you have very few visitors people will think that you are unpopular or not well known. It is best to ensure that the stat counter you choose to have has a good tracking service. This will show you where your visitors have come from and which pages they read and where they left your site. Having this information will help you target your advertising and see which pages are your most popular.

Think carefully about what literature you choose to use and order, it can be valuable to you but it is very expensive. Many people order brochures for their business during the very early months, but there are a couple of reasons why you may wish to wait:

* Test out your approach first through your website. There may be a package, or a service you offer that people don't understand and therefore you have an opportunity to change it
* Stationery is expensive and you could potentially benefit more by investing in internet advertising.
* Once someone has requested information from you they are looking for more personal information that suits them and their requirements – they've already read all about you on line.
* Most people will enquire by email, and if you have an electronic brochure you can email them, you will be able to respond to them quickly. Remember, they are likely to have asked many wedding planners for information – not just you, so the sooner you can respond with relevant and personalised information, the more chance there is of securing the booking.

The main literature you will need to buy is branded stationery – so business cards and letter headed paper. Shop around as there are some good offers with competitive prices available. If you have a good printer, you can print your own letter headed paper, just insert your logo onto the document.

Advertising

4

Your market research will help you to identify which websites you may want to advertise in and also give you an idea of whether you want to advertise in magazines and at wedding fairs.

There are two main types of advertising, Brand Advertising and Direct Response advertising.

Brand Advertising is done by the big companies such as McDonalds and Coca Cola. You know their logo immediately so their adverts can be subtle. This is not successful for the small to medium business, as people won't know who you are.

Direct Response Advertising is called this because, ultimately, you want a response (such as a call/email) directly because someone has read/heard/seen your advert and they want to know more.

It is absolutely essential that you measure your advertising success. If something doesn't seem to generate any interest then stop advertising in it.

You will always have to give something a go, but remember that the sales team are hired because they do a good job, and will persuade you to advertise for one more issue, but if its not working, invest your money in something else. When you take out adverts in magazines, always ensure that you understand the cancellation policy and dates, request amendments to this agreement if you want to so that you will be able to stop it quickly and not be tied in for six issues if it is not working for you.

Make sure that your website has a stat counter, you can have it hidden and not on display. This shows you the number of 'clicks' or visits that you have had, where they came from and how long they stayed. This is a good way of knowing what site your visitor came from, and on which webpage they left your site.

There's a classic formula used by advertisers and it is well worth remembering. The formula is AIDA. This stands for

Attention	*Desire*
Interest	*Action*

If you follow this formula in every advert that you write or place, you will increase your chances of success.

Attention – the first thing your advert needs to do is grab the reader's attention.

Interest – once you've got their attention, you need to create an interest in your service, and encourage the reader to want to know more.

Desire – There is a big difference between being interested in a service and desiring it. You need to convert the reader's interest into a strong desire for what you are offering. With Wedding Planning, this means convincing the reader that they need or could need your service.

Action - Even if someone desires what you have, it is not enough until they take action. At the end of the advert you need a call to action. Tell people exactly what they need to do next to get hold of you, and make it easy for them to do so. If you offer an incentive, and ask them to quote a reference, you will be able to see how successful your advert has been.

Once you've completed your website design, and you've started to write the text for your website, you need to really think about the messages that you want to tell. As mentioned earlier in this book, you should refer back to your business plan and your ideas for your business and consider the key messages. What it is about you that makes you good, unique, reliable and the wedding planner to choose?

Your advert should be a personal communication to the person reading it. It needs to be about them. It needs to address their needs, desires and fears and it needs to clearly tell them the benefits of what you are offering. Nobody will buy anything from you if they don't see a benefit from what you have to offer.

Research has shown that the best adverts are those which offer an impressive benefit to the reader. It should contain your business name and be quick to read (the media standard is about 4-8 seconds or about 15 words). You must keep it **quick, simple and to the point!**

Speak to your graphic designer about your ideas, but do try to use a clear layout, clear fonts and easy to read language.

When you've written your advert, imagine stepping into the shoes of your prospective customer. From this perspective does the advert fully convey what your message is? Would you want to know more?
If not, go back until it feels right.

4.1 Hints and Tips:

- ✤ Don't pay the full price at the outset – the sales person will normally be able to discount for you.
- ✤ Place your advert as close to the deadline as possible to ensure the lowest price
- ✤ Think about the best location for your advert, would your advert be better on the left hand page, if when you flick through magazines – you always look on the right hand page.
- ✤ Don't be bullied into advertising just because your competitors have advertised there.
- ✤ Ring other advertisers in the magazine/website and ask how they find the publication and if they generate many leads from their advert?

Having an advert in a magazine is good, having an editorial to go with it is even better. If you can get a mention in 'Editors Choice' or within the main part of a magazine it is so advantageous.

Try to give quotes and comments for articles and be a contributor to wedding magazines or wedding articles in the National Press, you are seen to be an 'expert'. This is invaluable, in terms of perception of you and your business, and can do nothing but good for your reputation.

A press release is a written or recorded communication aimed at members of the news media with the purpose of announcing something claimed to be news worthy. You should target your press release to editors at newspapers, magazines, radio and tv stations and follow it up with a call. A press release is different from a news article. A news article is a compilation of facts developed by journalists published in the news media, whereas a press release is designed to be sent to journalists in order to encourage them to develop articles on the subject. A press release is generally biased towards the objectives of the author.

Public Relation companies will use news releases. The aim of a news release is to attract favourable media attention to the PR firm's client. This provides publicity which attracts attention for the services and will generate interest.

You should write press releases as often as possible. To get them published they need to be newsworthy, include stats if you can and make them topical.

A template is included in the following pages.

Try to pre-empt news topics (remember when Prince Charles got married or Elton John?). When there is a high profile wedding on the cards – it's a perfect opportunity to get a lot of exposure.

Remember as well, that there has to be something in it for you and for the newspaper/magazine. They want an interesting article (and if possible free copyright photographs), and you want to make sure that they mention your company name in a favourable way. You may find looking at a website called 'press box' and seeing the press releases written there. You can search by industry, which will enable you to read previously written press releases in the wedding industry.

SAMPLE PRESS RELEASE

28 February 2009
For immediate release

THE SHOW MUST GO ON
Every Detail wedding planners open up new office in Cambridgeshire

Getting married in the middle of a recession is a challenging prospect to say the least, but help is on hand for engaged couples in the form of Every Detail Planning and Consultancy, a leading wedding planning business which has opened up an office in Cambridgeshire

Helping couples with everything from setting a budget for their big day, to arranging chair covers, the UK-wide company is looking forward to working with soon-to-be-wed's in the local area.

Barbara Collins "Now, more than ever, couples are looking to get the best deals and value for money when planning their wedding. Although it's tough out there for businesses, now is the time to grab bargains and negotiate cost-savings with suppliers, something that expert wedding planners at Every Detail are more than experienced at doing."

If you are planning a feature and need a comment from an expert wedding planner, please contact Barbara Collins on 07538 280023 for more information

Note to Editors:
Every Detail's professional wedding planners have been assisting brides and grooms in planning their weddings since 2001, both in the UK and abroad. For more information, please visit www.everydetail.co.uk

Barbara Collins, Every Detail
http://www.everydetail.co.uk weddings@everydetail.co.uk

# # #

Example Press Release Template

Date
FOR IMMEDIATE RELEASE:

Contact:
Contact Person
Company Name
Telephone Number
Fax Number
Email Address
Web site address

Headline
Town, County, Date — Opening Paragraph (should contain: who, what, when, where, why):

Remainder of body text - Should include any relevant information to your products or services. Include benefits, why your service is unique. Also include quotes from staff members, industry experts or satisfied customers.
If there is more than 1 page use:

-more-

(The top of the next page):
Abbreviated headline (page 2)
Remainder of text.

(Restate Contact information after your last paragraph):
For additional information, contact: (all Contact information)

Summarise service specifications one last time
Company History (try to do this in one short paragraph)

#
(indicates Press Release is finished)

Pricing your Services

5

At this stage we have spent time thinking about the kind of wedding planning company you would like to have. You have asked yourself

+ Will I concentrate on my local area or target further a field?
+ What kind of clientèle am I aiming for?
+ Will I do speciality weddings (such as 'green' or 'fair trade' weddings)?
+ Will I target the upper end of the market and have a minimum fee?

If you have done some research you will have an idea of how much some of the competition charge, and during the earlier work with the business case, you hopefully would have started to think about **'What will I do and how?'**

Spend some time thinking about it now – there are some questions below to help you think!

Activity

+ How should I price my services?
+ Will I want to offer 'set' packages?
+ What if people want to take some parts of a package out? Are separate elements costed so that I can work out the total price?
+ Will I offer some set packages and some more 'bespoke' prices?
+ Should I just charge a minimum fee?
+ Should I set a minimum on the value of the wedding budget? i.e. not work with anyone who has less than £40,000?

Once you have been able to give that some thought, you then may wish to begin thinking about the work that you did in the business plan about your company's running costs.

- ✥ How much does your web-hosting cost per annum?
- ✥ Internet connection per month/annum?
- ✥ Monthly phone bills? Land line and Mobile
- ✥ Stationery and printing?
- ✥ Advertising etc.?

These costs have to be recouped through the price that you charge. Therefore there does need to be some thought into how your price is calculated as you need to make the money to run your business, if nothing else.

Picking a figure out of the air, because it seems the right kind of price and is less or similar to your competitors isn't really the route to a long lived successful business.

Listed below are the most popular tried and tested approaches for charging your services. There are a number of pricing options that can be used and the suitability of these for both the bride and planner will depend very much on the certainty of what is required and what type of service is to be provided.

1) **Charge an agreed percentage of the bride's overall budget – this is a relatively common approach. You set a percentage (say 10%) of the wedding budget and charge this amount.**

Benefits - are that for a very large wedding with hundreds of guests in a very expensive venue will mean that you can earn a large fee.

Disadvantage - is that at the early stages this is an estimate. All of the suppliers and what they are providing is not defined and the agreed percentage may not fully cover all the activities that may need to be undertaken. This could lead to disputes on what is or not included and exposure on costs for the planner.

To consider - will you clearly state what is included for that % fee and what isn't? Is the budget set at the start, and be the amount that the percentage is allocated against? What happens if the budget goes over or under? Do you increase/decrease your fee? What if the couple feel that you purposely took them over budget to increase your earnings? How do you manage a change of scope (for instance, change of location after it's been booked – would you charge extra or is it all included?)

My Notes for this approach:

2) **Prepare the Proposal and Price for agreed scope & effort** – this is where you would understand and agree exactly what it is you are to do for them, and then provide a price that reflects that.

Benefits - the price that you charge will be a good estimate and should ensure that the payment you receive will be comparable to the time and effort that you put in. By clearly defining the work that you will undertake (scope) it will be easier for you to manage the relationship between you and your client and be sure that you are doing everything that they expect of you. You can also increase/decrease the price should the scope of agreed work change (especially whilst you negotiate the final cost). You should have a clearly written contract which details the work which will be carried out by you for the term of the contract.

Disadvantages - for couples with very small budgets, your fee could be the quite high in comparison to others, but will be a fair representation of the effor that you will need to give to plan their wedding. This approach is quite formal and for those clients that do book you, should they change their requirements and wish to add additional services they will incur a further expense which can affect the relationship.

To consider - how would you work out what to charge? Would you estimate the time it takes to do a particular task and then charge an hourly fee? How would you work out the minimum you need to charge to ensure that you recoup your running costs (i.e. phone/webhosting/internet etc.)?

My Notes for this approach:

3) **Charge on daily/hourly basis** – provide an invoice at the end of each month/period which invoices for the actual work (in time) that you have done

Benefits - this approach is useful for the early stages of a relationship when the couple don't know what they want, but want you to do some work for them. It is a good idea to agree to a short term piece of work and be clear on what it entails, to help them move to a position where they do know more clearly what they want and you can provide a quotation at that stage. Some people do just want help to get started, and when you are eager to win business you can provide a lot of your ideas and supplier contacts to try to 'win the deal'. The couple could decide to plan the wedding themselves and if you have provided all your information and your time for free then you will not receive any financial reward for your effort.

Disadvantages - it may seem expensive and couples may be reluctant to invest in the short term, when other planners offer a 'free consultation'. This consultation will not provide them with the tools, knowledge or research to decide where (location) and type of venue, or budget. If you don't agree a price for your initial work (especially if you feel that it will be more work than you usually offer for free) you are likely to do a lot of work for no reward, in the hopes that the couple may book you to plan their wedding.

To consider - what is an adequate hourly rate? How would you promote this approach to make it seem reasonable? Could you design a detailed proposal or 'beginning your plans' piece of work that would be a stand alone service to encourage more people to buy this approach from you – and therefore recoup money for all of your efforts?

Activity	My notes for this approach:

4)   **Fixed packages. This is where the planner offers two or three set packages that list the work/areas that they will do for a fixed price.**

Benefits - to this approach is that people who are looking at companies for comparisons can see clearly how much you cost and find this less daunting. You can mix and match your services to offer a choice and therefore meet the individual needs of your customers.

Disadvantages – what if people don't want everything in the package? How you will manage that, reprice and continue to make a profit. How can you build in additional costs like mileage, length of wedding day and planning time? Will potential customers look at your website and not know that there is some negotiation available and then go elsewhere as you don't match their needs completely?

Things to consider – you could offer a mix and match service, (such as a fee to do each element and then clients choose what they want). Or be clear on the scope – what you are and aren't doing, and show a price per hour/activity that you will charge on any activity in addition to that agreed. Likewise you should know how much to remove for a service that they don't want or need.

Activity	My notes on this approach:

It is very important to understand how you will price for your services, and be clear in your mind on this, as it will help you sell yourself successfully and you'll be less likely to make mistakes and charge unrealistic fees.

Whilst you are trying to determine the right approach for your company and your chosen audience, you may also wish to consider what the price should take account of and this may help you decide on the pricing approach that you take:

1) Customer's Budget and Cash constraints – ask them what they want to spend and you can create a proposal to meet their budget.

2) Certainty of scope – are you very clear on the amount of work you will need to do and be able to define this accurately before you start. You should get the clients' agreement at this stage.

3) Accurate and realistic estimates of effort required (i.e. how long will it take you?) so that you can work out your charges.

4) Your need to recover business overhead costs such as premises, insurance, running the business costs (phone, printing, mileage)

5) Supplier Quotations – you need to consider how you will work with suppliers (covered later in this manual). The big question is whether you provide your client with the quote direct from the supplier, or will you add on top or will you charge commission? You could consider charging the client less if this is the case.

6) Overall length of Contract – you need to consider the length of time that you are working with the client (over one or more years) and then decide whether you need to consider inflationary increases and the cost of money if payment is being made on a milestone basis and you won't receive some of it for some time. (ie. £10 today is worth £10 today but in 2 years time it is £12 after inflation).

7) Payment milestones and payment terms – will you ask people to pay a percentage of the overall fee on a timeline basis – such as 20% at the start 40% after 4 month, 30% after 10 months and remaining 10% 2 weeks prior to the wedding. It is advisable to use this or a similar approach to mitigate your risk of non payment in the case of cancellation or the couple running out of money.

8) Travel costs- location of the bride, venue and suppliers and number of likely visits needed, you should include these costs into your quote, unless you state that all mileage and expenses are charged separately.

9) Profit- unless your business plan allows for part funding activity then you must make a profit, so you will need to ensure that your overheads are well accounted for in your pricing strategy.

It is likely that you will have a few different ideas and you will need to think carefully on which you choose. Speak to friends and family about which they would feel most comfortable about if they were the client.

- ✣ Would they feel comfortable paying a large sum of money in advance of any work?
- ✣ Or how would they feel if they found out (as your client) that you put a mark up on each service or took commission.
- ✣ Would they want you to pay their suppliers on their behalf or pay them directly themselves?

If you, as the wedding planner, decide to make all payments to the supplier on the behalf of your client, then you should make sure you consider the bank charges you may incur for each payment received and made.

Contracts

6

Once the Bride and Groom have decided to proceed and want to work with you, a contract is needed. This formalises the relationship between you and ensures that the commercial and legal obligations and liabilities of both parties for the services to be undertaken are formally agreed.

It is important that you seek legal advice on the establishment of a set of Standard Terms and Conditions for Provision of Services, to ensure it provides you with adequate protection and that appropriate legal considerations are included, as well as references to current laws surrounding the sale of services.

The Contract will also provide protection of confidential data and trade secrets. If you are working with a celebrity couple (although this applies to all your clients) you need to ensure that you respect their confidentiality. This could be from the amount their wedding cost them; your fees; the fact that the Bride hates the Mother in Law to be, etc. By the end of your service, you will have formed a close relationship with the couple and are likely to know most of their thoughts and opinions on their guests and their suppliers.

Trade Secrets, and your professional knowledge, is all the information that you provide the couple during the term of your service. If you give them fact sheets, access to private areas of your website, your ideas and designs etc, you want to make sure that they don't share them with all their friends who then get married, or that they don't keep them and use them when starting up their own wedding planning business next year!

Your contract should also include clauses on termination (whether that be by you or your client). What will happen in the case of cancellation? You will need to be clear on how you will calculate what charge you will pass to the client if there is cancellation or postponement of the wedding, or if one of the suppliers cancel. Additionally, the contract should also cover poor performance (or non performance) in the case of third party suppliers and the liability of this (in other words whose fault will it be and who will give financial compensation).

Your contract should also include details on the payment terms (i.e. the time in which your invoices should be paid) and when the invoices will be raised and by whom. If you are dealing with a couple overseas or whose wedding is overseas, then you may wish to consider setting the exchange rate or using one banks exchange rate and referring to this in the contract.

The contract will need to be signed as two originals by both parties and retained by both parties.

Contracts are expensive, and some small business support organisations, such as the Federation of Small Businesses or Business Link may sell them to you.

Alternatively, the Wedding Training Company Limited and other wedding alliances and associations also sell contracts for wedding planning companies. You may need supplier contracts, and these are covered in the chapter under suppliers.

Working with Suppliers

7

7.1 Sourcing your suppliers

Suppliers are key to developing, planning and making the perfect wedding, and therefore choosing those that you wish to work with is a very important decision.

As such key contributors to your weddings, it is essential that you build a network of tried and tested suppliers that you can build good solid relationships with. However, not one wedding is the same so in addition to your "regular suppliers" you will also need to be able to source 'unknown' suppliers to meet a couple's individual wedding requirements.

It is therefore beneficial to attend trade shows and actively network with exhibitors and others in the wedding and event industries. There will always be household names, but in most cases it is the local dependable supplier that will provide the most cost effective service.

Build up a directory of suppliers and start to get to know them and their services and goods.

Give some thought to what you should look for in a supplier when you go out to meet them? What is important to you? How will you know you can trust them? Is the quality of their website/literature important?

Activity

The exercise above is to help you to determine what is important to you about the suppliers you choose. It is important, where possible, to meet with suppliers and discuss your company and theirs to begin to build a relationship and to make sure that you are happy to work with them – and recommend them to your customers.

Here are some additional questions to those you've thought of you may want to consider when you begin to meet with your potential suppliers. Likewise you may want to have given prior thought to some of the questions that they may ask you:

Questions for you to the supplier:

- How long have you been established?
- Have you had a part in many weddings?
- Do they have some photos you can use to demonstrate their capability?
- Do they have references from previous customers?
- Can you attend a wedding with them to see how they work?
- How can you work well together?
- What is their preferred style
- Is there a limit on how far they will travel

Likely questions from the supplier to you:

- How long have you been established?
- What did you do beforehand?
- Why did you choose to be a wedding planner
- How much will you charge for your services (You may not want to give a definite answer but a guide)
- Do you charge commission for referring a client to them?
- Will you add a charge on top of their fee?
- Who will the contract be between – the client and the supplier, or the supplier and you.
- Who will make the payments to the supplier? The client to the supplier or you to the supplier – having invoiced the client first. This will be dependent on your way of working, whether you charge a fee on top of the suppliers' quote.
- How will you work co-operatively together (it really is not about only selling them but them to actively promoting you too)

7.2 Selection Criteria

Reputation and Reliability

Part of the service that you offer is to recommend suppliers, it is essential that you have evidence of their reputation and reliability in their particular field. Seek references and examples of their capability, seek evidence from them of relevant accreditations and qualifications, and equally you may wish to establish their financial standing to ensure that they can deliver the commitments they have made (especially if you are making payments now for a wedding 18 months + away).

Sometimes, you may want to ask if they will do some work for you to show their capability – if a make up artist – do you a free trial, or is a florist make up some examples. If cars – look at them all, this is so that you are comfortable that the service they are providing is to the quality that you and your clients are expecting.

Value for Money

Notwithstanding that they may be providing a very unique service and quality may be of the highest level, but are they delivering you and your client value for money? Be prepared to challenge their proposals and seek quotes from alternative suppliers in order to compare on a like for like basis. Do not try to suggest to your clients that you will always be able to obtain discounted rates, or commission from the suppliers. Many just will not budge on their price, and why should they if they have priced at a realistic and sensible rate and even more so, if you have never worked with them before?

Pricing and Commercial Arrangements

You should request a formal quotation, so that you have a record of the prices discussed. It is essential that you provide the supplier with enough information, such as a document that details scope and delivery dates (before or on wedding date) against which they can offer a formal quotation.

It is often likely that some elements of the pricing will be fixed and some elements will remain variable, i.e. drinks subject to actual consumption, in which case you may need to guess on an estimated total for budget reasons, but make sure you make this very clear. Also, be very clear on whether or not the prices are inclusive or exclusive of VAT, and for which year the service is priced (for example, many wedding venues will send you the current year's pricing for a wedding in 18 months time, and their price is likely to increase before then, and the new price will be charged).

Proposals received should be checked (by you) against the requirements and should represent value for money, always clarify anything you are unsure of or that seems ambiguous.

Also give consideration to whether the supplier offered any discount based on your existing relationship; or on the basis of future opportunities for collaborating; because of low season; or on the basis of volume and quantity? It can be difficult to obtain discounts, but your primary objective should be that you are receiving value for money.

Equally you need to ensure that proposal pricing has a validity period that correlates with the wedding timescales i.e. quote valid until x date, on weddings between 'a' date and 'b' date. Are there any extras that have been included and/or excluded i.e. payment for samples/practice runs, expenses, VAT.

The formal agreement between planner and supplier should not only include pricing, payment and legal conditions, but also include obligations on the supplier to provide regular progress reporting and how communications with both bride and planner will be undertaken. In other words, will all communication be done through you, or will the supplier liaise directly with the client once the booking has been confirmed?

You should also be considering, who is the contract for the service between? Is the contract for the services being offered and bought between the bride and the supplier or the supplier and the wedding planner? Also, who will be making the payments – the bride directly to the supplier, or the bride to the wedding planner then to the supplier.

This choice is yours alone, and will form part of the business model you choose to follow. It is important that you consider at all times your liability, so what should happen if the bride's payment is late and you are charged interest on the bill from the supplier, or if your supplier increases their prices on a cost you have quoted to the client and you can't change your quote.

It is worth considering having standard contracts with your suppliers, especially if you are going to be using them time and time again. There is a supplier contract template in the template section of this manual. If you can have a supplier contract, which sets out clearly the services that you will procure, the timescales you need to provide to secure their services and the cost at which they are available, you can then freely quote their services to your clients, without needing to go back and forth all of the time. This is especially helpful for smaller items such as chair covers or linen.

Additionally, you may wish to have contracts with suppliers, especially if the contract is directly between you and them on a wedding by wedding basis that clearly stipulates the responsibilities of the wedding planner, the client and the supplier.

How to be a Wedding Planner

Case Example,
Wedding Planner, Every Detail, Wedding Planning and Co-ordination (www.everydetail.co.uk)

I had a wedding once, where the chair covers had been delayed by the courier. There were 150 guests at the wedding, and only 75 chair covers had arrived. The chair covers were for the civil ceremony and then again for the wedding breakfast.

With 2 hours to go until the ceremony began, the chair covers had not arrived and could not be traced by the courier company. Miles away from the supplier and couldn't get through to them on the landline or mobile, I began to call other chair cover suppliers within a 30 minute radius, which I thought would have given me time to speak to them, arrange delivery, and then put the chair covers on.

In the midst of this frantic telephone calling, the most local company had the chair covers, could supply them within 45 minutes, but wanted to double the price because of the predicament I was in. This forced me to stop and think and consider what the real issue would be if there were no chair covers. I went to the wedding file, which I had at the wedding and looked at the contract with the chair cover company. The clause stated that they were not liable, whether in fault or partly responsible for any failure to deliver the chair covers. Therefore, if I went ahead and purchased the chair covers I wouldn't be able to pass the cost back to the chair cover company, and would have been looking at a £375 invoice.

Due to the fact that there wouldn't be a way to offset the cost, I decided to take a decision, and put chair covers on the back rows, the aisle chairs and the front rows and hoped that the bride wouldn't notice! Thankfully, the chair covers were delivered 45 minutes before the ceremony started and I could put chair covers (without the sashes) on the remaining chairs before the ceremony started.

The biggest mistake I could have made would have been to order alternative chair covers and then either pay the costs out of my own funds, as the contract with the supplier said clearly that they weren't liable, or alternatively asked the bride to pay. My contract had stated that I wasn't liable for the third party performance. However, she could argue that the cost wasn't approved by her and therefore would be right to withhold payment.

Thankfully it all worked out, but the key lesson that I learnt was that you need to ensure that your contract will support you in every eventuality, and it pays to think of every worse case scenario to ensure that you are covered.

Recommending suppliers

If you are planning a wedding for your clients, from start to finish, then you should be offering your clients at least a choice of three suppliers. These should be within their price range and suit their requirements. Sometimes this can be very difficult, but you should try your hardest to give them a reasonable choice from which they can make a decision.

You should also begin to think about how you will present quotations received from suppliers to your clients. You should not forward quotes exactly as you have received them, but prepare the information so that they can see at a glance the key facts, which will include the price but probably isn't the deciding factor.

Clients have chosen to work with you to take the hassle away, to make it more time efficient, and to be able to make informed decisions on facts, rather than have to read copious amounts of paperwork and email before making a decision.

A template of how you may show this information to your clients is included in the appendix.

Courtesy of Stephanie Mackrill Photography – www.stephaniemackrill.com

Working with clients

8

During the early stages of setting up your business you may wish to consider writing and agreeing some 'key rules' that you abide by for your customers – such as replying to all emails within 24 hours; returning calls within 'x' hours; always offering a 'free' consultation..

Once you've received an enquiry from a prospective couple, you need to go and see them or speak to them in detail so that you can understand what it is they are looking for and whether you can assist them. Equally, this is your opportunity to sell yourself and promote your business, leaving them comfortable that you understand them and their ideas for their wedding day and would be able to work with them to make it happen. Ultimately, you want to encourage them to want to work with you.

8.1 ENQUIRY STAGE

Everyone knows how many seconds one has to impress new customers, and the importance of the initial enquiry, but what is very important to any bridal couple is that their wedding is important to you. That you are interested in it and that you want to assist them in making their day special and memorable. If it's treated as 'just another event' they are highly likely to walk away.

At the initial enquiry stage, you want to try and get as much information as possible, without being too questioning. It would help to know the date, possible number of guests, and whether they have already started to plan their wedding. If they have, what kind of wedding is it? You also want to know how much they already know about your company, your prices etc.

With this information, you're able to write to them to answer their enquiry. This is your opportunity to make it specific and ensure that you show that you listened, that you want their business and that you are proficient and capable. This letter should be personal, and should encourage them to meet with you.

Then with the information you've collated so far, and the initial meeting arranged, you can begin to prepare.

If you were the customer, and were looking to work with a wedding planner, what are the key qualities you would look for, and what would be important to you? List your ideas below:

A bride shares her reasoning here as to why she chose a wedding planner:

"When I was looking for a wedding planner about one year before my wedding, all I knew is that I didn't have the time or resources to plan a wedding overseas. In hindsight, I would tell any bride-to-be that it is well worth it. My fiancé and I talked about it, and aside from the support and comfort of having a wedding planner, I truly believe we would have spent more money than we planned.

Also, I am not a bride who has been planning or picturing my wedding since I was a little girl. So, I never paid much attention to everything that had to be done. I knew I needed help prioritizing and I didn't have a clue where to start. Furthermore, I wanted someone's help who was unbiased - someone who could tell me when something wasn't necessary, a poor idea, or out of the budget, and someone whose feelings I wouldn't hurt if I didn't agree with their idea.

At the beginning of the wedding planning process, I felt a little gluttonous hiring a wedding planner. I felt like having one was a luxury more than a necessity. I don't feel that way now; while it may be a luxury, it was well worth it and necessary. Several friends and co-workers have said to me, "what do you have to worry about, you have a wedding planner; she can just do it all for you." This is a complete misnomer in my opinion. A wedding planner does A LOT, but there are still a lot of things the bride and groom need to take care of themselves. I don't know how I would've done it all without help.

Finally, I haven't experienced the wedding itself yet, but in hiring a wedding planner, I knew I wanted someone who could help on the day of the wedding. There are so many people I don't get to see often, the last thing I want to do is run around making sure everything is in order. I am sure there will be some of this, but it would all be on my shoulders without help... and I just don't want to burden friends or family members. I want them to enjoy themselves as much as possible also".

Courtesy of Danni Beach Photography
www.dannibeachphotography.com

It is very important not to assume that people choose a wedding planner because they are unable to plan a wedding. This is a very common misconception. Instead, people that choose a wedding planner tend to be perfectly able to plan a wedding, but have limited time, and therefore see value in hiring a planner to do the legwork and keep the budget in shape, rather than just 'throw money at it', when they run out of time and are not able to do adequate research.

Following an enquiry, it is sensible to try to arrange a meeting so that they can make a decision about whether they wish to work with you or not. Likewise you will want to make the same consideration.

When brides and grooms look for a wedding planner, they tend to search the internet or do research. They then narrow down their list when they have received the wedding information through after their initial enquiry. Couples tend to have a list of key factors, which will help them decide on their chosen planner.

Key factors are listed below showing the most common that the couple will be looking to consider and compare (the order will differ):

+ Ability
+ Approach
+ Friendliness/Professionalism/Flexibility of the staff
+ Location
+ Price
+ Rapport
+ Reputation

Ability they will be looking to hear from you that you are capable in planning a wedding. The conversation wouldn't necessarily need to be you repeating yourself over and over that you can plan a wedding, but your ability will come through in conversation, the ideas you have, the recommendations you make, and more importantly, the confidence you show and the way you carry yourself.

Approach – everyone will approach the role of wedding planner differently, just the same as if you asked estate agents to view your home to sell it, they would all have a different approach. There's no 'right or wrong'.

The couple would like to feel assured that they'll receive value for money, a good service with a sensible approach. They would like to hear your ideas for keeping in contact, how you'll work together, meet suppliers, make decisions, etc.

Friendliness/Professionalism/Flexibility of the staff – like anything it is also about the people. How do you get on together? Do they like you? Can they imagine working with you for the next 12 months? It is best to be yourself, but not over familiar, be as you would in any professional environment, and ensure that you listen to the couple and what they want and make sure that any recommendations you make or ideas you share are relative and helpful.

Location – the couple will want to choose you because you either, live close to them, or close to their wedding venue. If neither of these then its because they trust you, and you will need to consider in your pricing the cost of travelling to meet both the client and liaising with the wedding venue(s).

Rapport – most couples will make their final decision based on who they preferred the most, and which wedding planner they 'connected' with the most, so do pay attention to them and their body language in the meeting and don't feel the need to just 'sell' yourself.

Reputation – it's difficult when you are first starting out to have a reputation and references, but it is worth ensuring that when you do 'get going' you have a mechanism for recording feedback to use as references and testimonials, and ensure you are able to get copies of photographs from weddings to use in your website gallery and portfolio if you have one. Also, don't under estimate the value of recommendations from other suppliers. If you can be recommended by local suppliers this will increase your reputation and encourage people to book you.

At the initial meeting (you'll need to think of a suitable location), try to find out through conversation the main elements of their wedding – such as number of guests, a date (is it flexible), how much they know about their type venue and style of wedding and how much money they have to spend.

You should at this meeting gain enough information for you to put a proposal together and price your services. It is worth asking if they have a budget in mind for what they want to spend on a wedding planner. In addition, you need to be able to tell them about yourself, your approach, how you work and the benefits of choosing you.

Set Expectations for both parties (Planner and client)

DO NOT SAY YOU CAN DO SOMETHING THAT YOU CAN NOT!

One of the most important lessons that you can learn in this manual, is never ever say that you can do something that you can't.

For instance:

- ✢ Save them the equivalent of your fees in discounts from suppliers
- ✢ Get them discounts from leading suppliers
- ✢ Exclusivity Arrangements
- ✢ Wonderful wedding for virtually no budget!

Once you've set their expectations you'll need to meet them.

You know what it is like, if you're having a dishwasher delivered for instance, and the company say it will be delivered between 8am and 12pm. You get up at the crack of dawn to be ready in case they come at 8, they eventually turn up at five minutes to 12. So you say, light heartedly to the delivery man, 'I've been waiting since 8', and he says, ' Oh no love, no way we'd have got to you for 8, you're the last one on the list of 20. To which, you think to yourself, well if they had said that I could have done x, y and z this morning.

Equally, if you say to a Bride, I'll send it to you next week, she'll be thinking, Monday – Oooh wonder if it's here yet, Tuesday, 'May be today', Wednesday 'Surely today' and by Thursday she'll be beginning to doubt your abilities, and start to have concerns about your professionalism and the 'state' of her wedding.

8.2 WRITING PROPOSALS

Proposals are written to a couple to outline what it is you can do for them, and what charge you will make. How you write and structure a proposal is certainly up to interpretation, and how you want to run your business. If you think about a situation at home, imagine you've asked for quotes for double glazing or an extension. You'd have met with a selection of suppliers and then asked them to provide you with a quote.

When you get the quote, you'll be checking that they've listened to you, priced for what you want and ONLY what you want. Ideally as well, you would want to know their timescales and maybe some references, and evidence of previous work.

When writing your proposal to the client, it is your decision how much information you decide to put in there. Some companies put in design ideas, suggested suppliers, and possibly mood boards of their ideas. If you choose to do this, it is all your effort and time, so you may want to consider charging to prepare the proposal.

The key elements of any proposal should be:

- ✣ Acknowledgement of the information they gave you (date, location)
- ✣ What you understand they require from your services,
  and how you will work with them to deliver it
- ✣ What you are quoting for (you will have thought about this and your 'approach'
  when you did your business plan and designed your business)
- ✣ The price that you want to charge (think about mileage costs, length of time, etc.)
- ✣ Overview of your terms and conditions

Once you've sent it to the client (if you email you should still send one in the post), invariably people are going to negotiate or question the price, so you'll need to understand how you got to it. You will also need to consider what you will discount by if they ask for you to do so.

Ultimately the idea of the proposal is to win you the business, but at the same time your price needs to be reasonable, and enable you to make a living.

8.3 Working together

Once the client has agreed to your price and you have agreed between you the 'scope' of work (i.e. agree everything you will do for them, within which timeframe and for how much) then you need to get on with planning their wedding.

You may wish to put a plan together. This could be relatively high level with a timeline showing every 3 months, and then the suppliers to be researched and booked in that timeframe. Or, you could be a lot more detailed and break it down to monthly or weekly tasks.

In the early stages of working together, you'll discover the best way to work and find how you best communicate, whether it's weekly telephone calls, emails or regular meetings. It is worth agreeing how you will provide regular updates so that you set expectations early on, you will be clear that it is unlikely that you won't be in touch every day and also that you will be working on the wedding, but will provide timely updates so that they remain feeling involved and consulted.

You may feel that a weekly phone call, or fortnightly update email is too often, but you can always think of something to say, even if it's questions for them. If you have regular updates arranged it will help you schedule your workload and arrange the meetings that you need to attend to gather information. This will become obvious to you when you are actually working on the wedding, and you will be thinking about the length of time to plan their wedding. If it is 6 weeks from booking you through to the wedding day, then you may wish to speak to the couple twice a week. If the wedding isn't until 18 months away, then you may agree formally to speak once a month, but during busier times, you will be communicating much more frequently.

When you're with your client, pay attention to their body language. If you fail to pick up on hints and polite refusals to suggestions, they will then think that you don't listen, don't care, or have an ulterior motive (especially if you take commission or are on a percentage payment arrangement).

Make sure you ask them lots of questions to ensure that you understand their requirements and what they want. If they don't like things that you have suggested, that's fine, ask what it is about it they don't like and you can eliminate that aspect from your search/ideas/recommendations.

Remember that it is their wedding. If they want their parents to sit at the back of the room, then that is their choice. You can offer suggestions and advice but it is their wedding. NOT YOURS! You can never, ever become too emotionally involved, nor at anytime say 'I'd really like that': on a bad day they may take it the wrong way and get upset. Likewise, if you are newly married, they don't want to hear about your day. As tempting as it may be, brides to be don't want a wedding planner who has just got married and talks about their own day all the time. They will either think that you're only a planner as you want to do it all again, or that you are comparing your wedding to theirs. If you must talk about your wedding and it is relative, then you can refer to it as a wedding that you had planned.

Every now and again, take a step back, and imagine you were a guest. Would they notice – and be upset, if the bridesmaids weren't all wearing the same eye shadow and lipstick?

Will the guests mind having to wait until 8pm for their meal when the ceremony was at 2pm? It is worth regularly looking at the arrangements from the eyes of the guest or supplier to make sure that it makes sense and doesn't present a problem.

What will make the difference?

This is why the couple chose you, and why they pay you. What is it you, as their wedding planner, are offering them from the service you provide to make you worth your wage and your ideas. You want their guests, their family and them to say, our wedding planner was amazing and so well worth it.

Many people choose a wedding planner as they think that they are guaranteed a beautiful, memorable and inspirational wedding.

One which has the 'wow' factor.

What is the 'WOW FACTOR'? It is different to many people, what does it mean to you? On the following page, record the ideas that come into your mind, regarding weddings, when you think about the 'wow factor'. What ideas would you begin to think of that you could recommend to your clients?

Activity

What is the 'WOW' factor?

For me, I think that the 'wow factor' is the one thing that either, makes your Bride and Groom's day, what will they look back on in 5 years' time and think 'WOW so glad we did that!'. Or it's the surprise of the guests when they see something they weren't expecting. This could be the room layout when they first see it, a firework display, singing waiters, magician or a combination of the whole day.

A day that surpasses anything that they had ever imagined, but is within their budget, their remit and is what they wanted!

Wedding Law and Restrictions

9

Understanding wedding law, and any restrictions that are in place is imperative during the very early stages of your wedding planning. This section is based on English Law (not including Scotland). If you are planning a wedding outside of England, then your first port of call should be to look at the country's law, and then look at the Embassy website of the nationality of the couple, in the country of the wedding. For example, if the couple are British, but want to marry in Italy, then you would go to the British Embassy website in Italy. It will provide you with the initial information that you must comply to.

Courtesy of Danni Beach Photography
www.dannibeachphotography.com

In England the law states that the Bride and Groom MUST:

- ✢ Be over 16
- ✢ Have parental consent if they are between 16 and 18
- ✢ Be married between 8am and 6pm
- ✢ Have 2 witnesses present
- ✢ Not be closely related
- ✢ Be of sound mind when the wedding takes place
- ✢ Meet the residency requirement
- ✢ Choose an approved venue which:
- ✢ Has a licence (if not a Church)
- ✢ Be within their Parish (if a Church)
- ✢ Is open to the public
- ✢ Holds the wedding indoors
- ✢ The venue must be fixed (i.e. – a ship at sea - it would have to be permanently moored)
- ✢ Must be suitably solemn

Wedding Law and Legal Restrictions really are not the most fascinating part of wedding planning, but it is an area that you must understand. It is one area where most couples make assumptions very early on, such as they want to get married in the pretty country Church near where they go to the pub each Sunday for lunch. Usually you will be the one to shatter that dream and if you don't manage their misconceptions from the start – you'll have some real explaining to do later on.

In order to marry legally within the laws of the England you must:

- ✤ Not be married to someone else
- ✤ Not be related by blood, adoption or marriage to each other within certain specific degrees (if you are uncertain – call your local registry office for advice)
- ✤ Be in possession of the correct documentation
- ✤ Give notice to the Registrar, Priest or Minister at the right time
- ✤ Pay the correct fees
- ✤ Live in the Registration District that you wish to get married in, or be marrying someone who lives in that district
- ✤ Meet the Minimum Residency Requirement - 15 days prior to giving notice of the intended marriage to the registrar or minister.
- ✤ Either have the Banns read or obtain the appropriate certificate
- ✤ Ensure that the ceremony takes place between the hours of 8am and 6pm, in a properly licensed place
- ✤ The ceremony must be performed and registered by an appropriately licensed person
- ✤ Have 2 independent witnesses
- ✤ Make sure that they collect a copy of the entry in the Registrar's book of Marriages (Marriage Certificate) after the ceremony

There are restrictions on who can marry who. If the couple are related by blood then they aren't allowed to marry. Cousins can marry, but adopted siblings can't. The table below lists who can not marry who.

For Men	For Women
Mother	Father
Grandmother	Grandfather
Daughter	Son
Granddaughter	Grandson
Aunt	Uncle
Niece	Nephew
Sister	Brother
Any person registered as a male at birth	Any person registered as a female at birth
Daughter in Law *	Son in law*
Mother in Law*	Father in law*
Step-Daughter*	Step Father*
Step-Sister*	Step Brother*
Adopted Sister*	Adopted Brother*
Adopted Daughter*	Adopted Son*

*relationship where marriage may be possible in certain circumstances.

How to be a Wedding Planner

Do not get confused between a marriage and a Civil Partnership. A Civil Partnership allows two people of the same sex to 'get married'. It is a legal ceremony which enables same sex couples to gain formal recognition of their relationship and have similar rights as married couples.

People who have lived in the same household as relatives are not permitted to marry, even though there may be no blood relationship. There are only two sets of circumstances where this is possible:

- ❖ If the elder of the two people was over 18 years of age when the step-relationship began
- ❖ If the two people have not actually ever lived together in the same family home and both will be over 21 when the marriage is due to take place

Marriage between a man and his daughter-in-law/mother-in-law or between a woman and her son-in-law/father-in-law is possible and both are over 21 and widowed.

If you are still unsure of the situation and require further clarification of whether the couple can or cannot marry, contact a registrar. You can usually find details of the local register office under the entry of Registration of Births, Deaths and Marriages on your local Government's website.

WHERE CAN THEY MARRY?

Most religions and faiths have special places set aside for worship and the performance of marriages. Not all of these ceremonies and places are recognised in civil law and therefore would mean that the marriage may not be legal. If this is the case ,then you would have to investigate additional options to enable the formal element of the wedding to happen.

In order to conform to the law in England, Northern Ireland and Wales, (Scotland is different) the place and person must be licensed. The ceremony must take place in daylight (between 8am and 6pm). In Scotland, only the registrar must be licensed so the wedding can take place in any suitable building.

Only Church of England ministers and registrars are licensed persons. Other places of worship of other religions (Christian, Buddist, Muslim, Hindu, Jewish), or the local Registry Office and other premises (such as hotels) can request the appropriate licence to be able to perform wedding ceremonies.

Some faiths and religions and their places of worship, may not be licensed and therefore having their wedding there would not be legal and the marriage would not be legally recognised. In this case, you would need to recommend that the couple are married in a Registry Office (or other licensed premises) and then have a blessing in their chosen place of worship.

RESIDENCY REQUIREMENTS

You will hear the phrase 'residency requirements', especially if you are assisting a couple to get married outside of their parish/registration district or if they will to get married abroad. Residency Requirement means, how long the couple wishing to marry need to be in the country (registration district) before the wedding. For some countries – such as Scotland, there isn't one, for other places such as New York or Italy it is very short – 1 to 3 days.

Each country has its own requirements and they form part of the rules of that land. The requirements will state the period of time that a couple need to be living in the country for before they can get married. Some countries have a very short residency period, others like the UK, France or Spain, are very long and make it virtually impossible for couples that don't live in the country to be married there. You can easily find this information on the British Embassy website for weddings abroad, or for non-British nationals wishing to marry in the UK.

Part of the process of giving marriage requires the couple to 'Give Notice' this commences the civil marriage proceedings and is the equivalent to the Banns being read.

The Immigration and Asylum Act 1999 introduced changes to the Marriage Act 1949. These changes came into effect on 1 January 2001.These changes consist of:

- ✤ A common 15 day notice procedure
- ✤ A requirement for each party to the marriage to personally give notice of intention to marry
- ✤ A requirement for each party to the marriage to declare their nationality
- ✤ Powers to request evidence of identification by the Superintendent Registrar
- ✤ In order to be married in England, each of the couple must have lived in a registration district in England or Wales for at least **seven days** immediately before giving notice at the register office. After giving notice they must wait a **further sixteen days** before the marriage can take place, (for example, if notice is given on 1 July the marriage may take place on or after 17 July).

If you are working on behalf of a couple wishing to marry in England or Wales, that don't live here, they **must satisfy** the residential qualification of **7 days and then wait a further 15 clear days** before they will be eligible to marry. In all cases check with the Registrar in that district.

The Registrar General for England and Wales interprets a 'day' as spending a night in the registration district in which you give formal notice of your marriage. A 'night' means a 'whole night in which you slept', that is, spending the whole night and not just part of it in the registration district in which you intend qualifying for the residency requirement.

England and Wales are split up into registration districts. It is possible to give your notice in one district yet marry in another.

<u>Giving Notice for Couples not living in England or Wales</u>

If you are assisting a couple to get married in England and Wales, who are not living in the area, then you should ensure that the couple write to the Register Office where they will be giving notice of their marriage, giving details of their travel arrangements and intended marriage date.

The Superintendent Registrar will then confirm that the arrangements are satisfactory (from a timing point of view) and will make an appointment for them to give formal notice and also a provisional booking for the marriage ceremony. Often, the Registrar will see them if they are on a visit to the UK, and be able to use this meeting as part of the formal process.

Evidence of Meeting the Residency Requirement

When your couple give formal notice of their marriage, they will be required to sign a declaration that they meet the residency requirement. Both of them will be required to declare their nationality. This is to enable the Superintendent Registrar to advise whether any further administrative procedures or legal requirements are needed to ensure the registration of the marriage in their own country.

Normally the preferred document as evidence of nationality will always be a passport, and it is likely other documents will be required as well – such as birth certificate and any change in name or divorce papers. In the absence of such a document, advice should be sought from the Superintendent Registrar in the district where the notice is to be given.

Wedding Ceremony

If you followed the wedding of Prince Charles to Camilla Parker-Bowles, you would have seen that it is not possible to choose a venue that you would like to get married in, and assume that this is legal. They chose Windsor Castle, and didn't realise that it needed to be a licensed venue and so subsequently ended up at the local Registry Office!

In England, there are 2 places you can be legally married. Either a Church, which has been sanctioned to carry out marriages, or a venue which has been licensed to hold a civil wedding. This could either be a hotel, stately home or a Registry Office. Many Registry Offices are very nice, well decorated and are a good choice if they are close to the wedding reception venue.

Courtesy of Danni Beach Photography
www.dannibeachphotography.com

10.1 REGISTRY OFFICES

Many couples are reluctant to consider marrying in a Registry Office as they perceive them to be drab and dreary places where you only get married if you really have no other choice. This may have been the case a couple of generations ago, but it certainly isn't the case any more. Registry Offices tend to now have modern, well decorated rooms and are often in well kept grounds that are suitable for photographs. It is worth considering viewing the couples' local Registry Offices to see what they are like and whether they would be a suitable option. If budget is tight, then looking at Registry Offices in the vicinity (there are usually a few to compare if you look in neighbouring districts) is a good option, as the fees to get married in a Registry Office are usually much less than elsewhere as they won't have to pay for venue hire costs.

As we have previously discussed, you can get married on any day of the week between 8am and 6pm. Most Registry Offices are only open from 10am-4pm Monday to Friday and 10am-1pm on Saturdays. If you are looking to arrange a ceremony outside of the Registry Office hours (but within the permitted hours), then you will have to arrange the ceremony to take place at a licensed venue (an approved premise).

Since April 1995, it has been possible to arrange for civil ceremonies to take place at certain venues other than a Registry Office. These other venues are officially known as approved premises but are more commonly known as licensed wedding venues. Locations such as Stately Homes, Castles, Hotels and the Local Football Club, can now be licensed to allow civil marriage ceremonies to take place on their premises.

The legal requirements for getting married at a Licensed Venue are the same as those at a Registry Office but it is your responsibility to arrange for a registrar's attendance at the venue. It is not necessary to give formal notice of the marriage to the Superintendent Registrar of the registration district in which the approved premise is situated.

However, after making a provisional booking of their chosen venue, you should immediately contact the local Superintendent Registrar since their attendance is required for the solemnisation of the couple's marriage.

Once you have ensure availability and booked the Superintendent Registrar, you can then confirm the booking at the chosen venue.

Wedding Venues can perform marriages during the full period of time allowed for marriages to take place; which is on any day between 8am and 6pm (including Sundays, Public and Bank holidays). This means, that they could potentially be more than one wedding on a wedding day, especially if they have more than one room which is licensed to perform a wedding ceremony.

The marriage ceremony at a Registry Office and a licensed venue must have no religious content whatsoever. However, in a licensed venue, there is the opportunity to personalise the ceremony more than in a Registry Office and it can be as formal or casual as the couple wish.

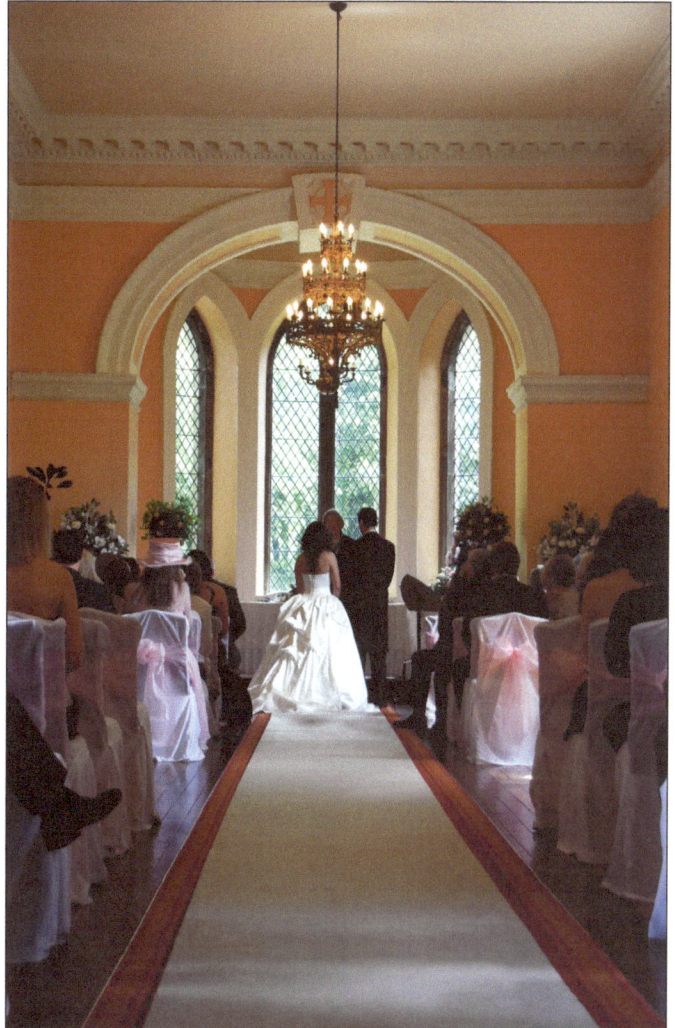

Courtesy of Alison and Steve Forrest, Elmcroft Studios www.elmcroftstudios.com

You can only change or individualise a standard civil ceremony by having their own choice of non-religious music and readings with the permission of the attending Registrar. Likewise, they (you) should also confirm that it is permissible for them to have their ceremony photographed or videoed. It is also possible for the couple to have their own choice of vows and promises that have a special meaning, although these will be in addition to the statutory words that are required to be said for the marriage to be legal.

Marriages in the Church of England and Church in Wales are governed by the Marriage Act, 1949. As the established church, the Church of England gives all British citizens, with no former partner still living, the right to get married in the parish Church where they are resident or in the Church where either of the couple are on the Church's electoral roll (not the local register of electors)

The couple do not have to be regular churchgoers to get married in the Church of England or Church in Wales, neither must they have been baptised. Both Churches welcome the opportunity for couples to make their solemn promises to each other.

The Church of England had for sometime been considering relaxing the restrictions around where people can marry. Previously, marriages were only allowed in the Parish Church. A working group was set up by the Church called The Marriage Law group, and they began to look at ways in which they could change in order to support the Government's proposals to reform the civil registration system.

In July 2007, the General Synod passed the Church of England Married Measure which came into force on the 1st October 2008. The measure hoped to update the law and restrictions on where one can marry to try and meet the changes in society. We know, that people are no longer born, married and die in the same Parish. The Measure does not change the existing right of parishioners; they can still be married in their parish church, where one or both of them are registered and on the electoral roll.

It does acknowledges that some people wish to marry in a Church because it has special significance for them, even though it is not where they live. This measure enables a church to offer the opportunity to have their marriage there if they can demonstrate a straightforward connection with the parish, without the couple having to apply for a special licence.

The object of the Measure is to grant couples the same right to marry in the parish church of a parish with which one or both of them can demonstrate a "qualifying connection" of a kind specified in the new legislation as a person resident in the parish would have.

A person has a Qualifying Connection with a parish if:

that person:

- was baptised in the parish. (This does not apply where the Baptism formed part of a combined service of Baptism or Confirmation); or
- had his or her Confirmation entered in a church register book of a church or chapel in the parish; or
- has at any time had his or her usual place of residence in the parish for at least 6 months; or
- has at any time habitually attended public worship in the parish for at least 6 months;

or a parent of that person has at any time during that person's lifetime:

- had his or her usual place of residence in the parish for at least 6 months; or
- habitually attended public worship in the parish for at least 6 months;

or a parent or grandparent of that person was married in the parish.

This only applies to the Church of England. A copy of the Marriage measure legislation can be found on the www.opsi.gov.uk website

The Marriage Measure offers the Church an opportunity to clarify, reissue and offer a wider welcome to couples who are requesting Church weddings.

Church Marriage of Divorcees

The Church of England, does marry divorcees, and whilst a minister of the Church of England does have a legal right under civil law (by virtue of his role as a registrar) to take a marriage service, regardless of whether or not either of the couple is a divorcee, the Minister may choose to discuss the previous marriage, and the circumstances that led to the separation and divorce and decide not to marry the couple. In many cases, parish priests are obliged to conform to their Bishop's policy of not allowing divorcees (whose former partner is still alive) to remarry in church.

If the parish priest refuses to perform the marriage, there is no process of appeal. Priests are also within their rights to refuse to allow their church to be used for this purpose by another 'sympathetic' priest.

10.4 CHURCH OF ENGLAND WEDDINGS – WHAT TO KNOW

Typically, Church weddings are held on a Saturday, although there is no legal reason why a wedding cannot be on a Sunday in a Church. However, it is usually not possible because the minister's day is too full with the normal Sunday services. Sometimes a minister/Priest may refuse marriages during Lent, and often during Advent. Lent is the period of time leading up to Easter Sunday and is traditionally the time when Christians abstain or take up something that spiritually or physically cleanses the mind or body. Its also worth remembering that during Lent, there are little or no flower decorations in the Church.

There are four ways of getting married in accordance with the rites of the Church of England:

- ✢ by publication of Banns
- ✢ by common licence
- ✢ by special licence issued by the Archbishop of Canterbury
- ✢ by the authority of a Superintendent Registrar's certificate without licence

There is usually little involvement in this legal side of the arrangements. The couple will be advised by their parish priest on the most suitable approach for them to follow according to their circumstances. If the couple are British subjects living overseas, you could either ask their parents to see the priest of the parish in which they lived or go yourself on their behalf.

Publication of Banns

Publication of Banns, is a legal term, which means announcing the intended marriage. This is the traditional method used by most couples who are marrying in a Church, and is equivalent to the civil method of getting married by certificate. The Banns are published by being read aloud during the service on three successive Sundays preceding the wedding ceremony. The purpose of doing it is so that the congregation are able to register objections, if they have any. It is usual for the couple to be in attendance on at least one of the three occasions when the Banns are published.

If the couple live in different parishes, then the Banns will need to be published in both parishes. A certificate stating that the Banns have been published will be issued by the Church that will not be holding the ceremony. This certificate needs to be produced to the officiating minister before the ceremony can proceed. If the marriage does not go ahead within three months of the Banns being published, the Banns will have to be published again.

Marriage by Common Licence

Should your clients, for some reason, not be able to meet the residency requirements and have their Banns read prior to their proposed wedding ceremony, then they could apply to be married by Common Licence.

A Common Licence application has to be approved by the Bishop of the diocese in which they wish to marry (or by one of his surrogates), and only one clear day's notice is required before the ceremony can take place.

The only residence requirement is that at least one of them must have lived in the parish during the 15 days leading up to the application for the licence. To be married by common licence, at least one of them must have been baptised. A common licence lasts for three months from its date of issue.

There must be a good reason for requesting a common licence, for example, an imminent and unavoidable departure overseas that prevent the banns from being read. A common licence is usually applied for by British couples who are no longer resident in England or Wales or if one or both of the couple are not British subjects.

Marriage by Archbishop of Canterbury's Special Licence

Marriage by Special Licence is very unusual and it must be approved by the Archbishop of Canterbury. The Licence is issued from the Registrar of the Court Faculties in London. A Special Licence allows a marriage to take place at any time within three months and in any place without any residence requirement. Typical reasons for getting married by special licence are when a couple want to get married in a parish where neither of them live, or if one of them is very ill in hospital and cannot be moved to a venue where marriages can be legally solemnised. To be married by Special Licence, at least one of the couple must have been baptised..

The benefit of getting married by Special Licence is that there is no residency requirement and so therefore is an option for couples living overseas, particularly if one or both of them had close links with the church in which they intend to marry. However, the agreement to issue a Special Licence is at the discretion of the Archbishop of Canterbury and it may well be that the recommendation will be that the couple should get married by common licence, which will require at least one of them to meet the residency requirement of 15 days. A Special Licence will be refused if neither of the couple is able to demonstrate a genuine and long standing connection with the church in question.

Marriage by Superintendent Registrar's Certificate without Licence

The only other option available to get married in the Church of England is by the authority of a Superintendent Registrar's Certificate without Licence.

This is for the marriage of qualifying relatives-in-law. If this is approved, the Church where the marriage is to take place must be located in the same registration district as the Register Office that issues the certificate.

Additionally, one of the couple must have lived in the parish for seven days prior to giving notice. Then for twenty-one days after giving notice, a certificate of authority to get married will be issued. The marriage must take place within 12 months from the date the notice was entered in the notice book.

10.5 ROMAN CATHOLIC WEDDINGS

For couples that are both Roman Catholic, the publications of Banns will be read out at the weekly service. However, hey do not form part of the legal preliminaries. If only one of the couple is Roman Catholic, Banns are not published and the priest will have to give permission for the marriage to take place either in a Roman Catholic Church or a non-Roman Catholic Church.

In order to be legally married in a Roman Catholic Church, the same legal requirements that apply to civil marriages, also apply to a Roman Catholic wedding ceremony. However, if the Church is in a different registration district than where the couple live, they will need to prove to the Superintendent Registrar that the Church is their normal place of worship. If they cannot do this, they will be required to give notice in the registration district in which the Church is situated after having met the necessary residency requirement.

The Priest at the chosen Church will be able to talk through the process and will make it very straightforward, and it is likely that the couple will have little idea the process was different than a Church of England Wedding.

10.6 Jewish Weddings

Civil law allows Jewish weddings to take place anywhere, for example, in a synagogue, private house, hired venue or even outdoors. Rabbinical law requires that a Jewish ceremony is performed under a chuppah (a wedding canopy). Jewish ceremonies can also take place at any time except on the Sabbath (Saturday) and on festival or fast days.

There are legal requirements to be followed for a Jewish wedding ceremony and, again, they are the same as those that apply to civil marriages. If the synagogue is in a different registration district to where the couple live, then they will need to prove to the Superintendent Registrar that the synagogue is their normal place of worship. If they cannot do this, then they will be required to give notice in the registration district in which the synagogue is situated after having met the necessary residency requirement.

If there is no synagogue in their registration district, they will be permitted to marry in a synagogue in the nearest registration district that has one (subject also to the approval of the synagogue secretary).

A Superintendent Registrar will only need to attend the ceremony if the secretary of the synagogue is not licensed to keep a marriage register. If this is the case, then arrangements should be made as far in advance as possible, as you can not guarantee the Superintendent Registrar's availability. An addition sum will also be payable for the registrar's attendance.

10.7 Nonconformist Church Marriages

Any marriage taking place in a Church, other than in the Church of England, will need to follow similar procedures to marriages in the Roman Catholic Church, ensuring compliance to the legal requirement which apply to civil marriages.

Again, if the church is in a different registration district to where the couple live, then they will need to prove to the Superintendent Registrar that the church is their normal place of worship. If they are unable to do this, then they will be required to give notice in the registration district in which the church is situated after having met the necessary residency requirement.

If there is no church of their chosen denomination in the registration district in which they live, then they will be permitted to marry in a church in the nearest registration district that has one.

A Superintendent Registrar will need to attend the ceremony if the minister is not authorised to register marriages, and therefore you should ensure of their availability. If the church in which they intend to marry is not registered for the solemnisation of marriages, then they must arrange for a civil ceremony beforehand to comply with the requirements of the law.

10.9 Muslim, Hindu and Sikh Marriages

UK Law has allowed for mosques and temples to be registered for the solemnisation of marriages according to the rites of these religions. Like in previous paragraphs, the process is the same as that for a civil wedding and the couple will be required to give notice of their intention to marry in the residency area in which they live. If the building is not in their registration district then they must prove that they meet the required residency requirement. If there is no building in their registration district then they can marry in the next closest.

Other Types of Weddings and the Service

Activity

What kind of weddings can you think of, which may have a different approach or aspect to it? Are there any you think you may need to research further to ensure you understand the legal requirements?

Some you may have had in your list:

- ✤ Second marriages
- ✤ Methodist/Baptist Weddings
- ✤ Jewish Weddings
- ✤ Quaker Weddings
- ✤ Muslim Weddings
- ✤ Civil Weddings
- ✤ Naval Weddings
- ✤ Humanist
- ✤ Same sex
- ✤ Roman Catholic
- ✤ Greek Orthodox
- ✤ Military
- ✤ ….and so the list continues

From the thinking that you've done, you will see that there are many types of marriages, and whilst you may not be expected to be an expert in all, it is very important to have an overview of the wedding traditions and processes and to be able to be sympathetic to the required elements of the service whether it is your chosen religion or not.

It would be wise to learn as much as possible before meeting with the couple about their type of service and then let them 'fill in the gaps' as time progresses, rather than go to the first meeting with them uninformed and they spend considerable time explaining their traditions to you.

Wedding & Reception Venues

11

One of your first activities during the wedding planning process is to work with the couple to find a wedding venue, whether it be for the whole day or the ceremony in one location and the reception in another, sometimes, there may be two reception locations, so you could be looking for up to three locations.

It is advisable to offer a selection of venues to a couple which vary slightly as knowing what they don't like is just as important as what they do. Many couples have a good idea what they are looking for, but it is very rare that they can tick all of their boxes when looking for a venue.

For some money isn't a problem, but for the majority it is.

Initially the couple are looking for a venue that looks good, and they can see their 'theme' (if they have one) in. For this it is best if the venue has a room that can be dressed easily. Weddings are predominately romantic affairs and whilst one would probably not admit it, they want a venue that will impress their guests.

Your first activity would be to talk to the couple and get a really good feel for what they want, and give some guidance at that stage on what kind of venue they will get for the budget they have.

During this time you would look for venues that fit their requirements and shortlist those suitable. You would, at the same time, check the costs and associated charges to ensure that everything you recommend is affordable.

Often venues can be slightly over their budget, in which case you'll need to look for areas to save money. Either from within the venue and catering costs – such as providing their own champagne or wine and paying the corkage charge, or by amending the menu to replace dessert with wedding cake. This is where the 'flexibility' of the venue becomes important, whilst it's appreciated that you can't get a discount on everything, there are normally a couple of items that you negotiate on.

Other items that will make venues more appealing are either additional discounts or 'free' items, such as a free bedroom or discounted rates with local hotels, deals with suppliers such as florists or chair cover hirers.

When looking at the cost of the venue, you should be looking at the overall cost and then comparing, rather than comparing like for like – such as main meal cost at one venue against the cost of a main meal at another, as they may price completely differently. One may charge one cost per person and include in that price all the food and drink, as well as a Toastmaster, chair covers and DJ, whilst another may charge for all items individually such as room cost, welcome drinks, canapés, wedding breakfast, wines etc. The second could look much cheaper at first glance. Therefore you should work out total costs for each venue for your clients to make an informed decision.

What do people look for in a venue?

Couples do not choose their venue by price alone, the bullet points below give an insight into some of the thoughts a couple may have on venues when they start to look at venues for their wedding day. Do remember that this is the first activity they are likely to do in the planning process, so are likely to be very idealistic and not as willing to compromise as they will be later on in the planning process.

Courtesy of Alison and Steve Forrest, Elmcroft Studios – www.elmcroftstudios.com

Design and Appeal

✤ Is it visually appealing? Will it need a lot of decorating?
✤ Does it fit with their theme?
✤ Will it impress their guests (even the website/brochure)?
✤ Cost and Flexibility
✤ Is there a corkage charge?
✤ Can they choose their own menu? Substitute dessert with cake?
✤ What is included in the 'package' or is it individually priced?
✤ Wow Factor
✤ What are the additional extras?
✤ Fireworks
✤ Amazing photo opportunities
✤ Special Offers
✤ Free 'dressing room' for bride and groom
✤ Discounted local hotel rates
✤ Are the table centres/chair covers/red carpet included
✤ Is the DJ included in the price

Venue Showrounds

When you have shortlisted venues for your clients to review, they will take some time to look through them, and then are likely to choose a shortlist which they will want to spend some time to visit.

You will be expected to make appointments to see your clients chosen venues, ideally you would want to be there and see the location with them. Depending on how much you have charged for your services, you may wish to visit the venue in advance to make yourself familiar and meet the venue's event planner, and then accompany the couple to see the venue as well so that you are able to see their reaction and understand their decision on which venues they like and those they don't – and what you need to look for if none were suitable.

If you choose to show clients around the venue then you will need to be knowledgeable about the venue and:

- Point out the selling points
- Understand the costs of the venue and what impact it has on their budget
- Refer to previous successful weddings when sharing relevant ideas
- Look into marriage law and local marriage venues

As mentioned previously, it is advisable that you've seen the venue before and have begun to form a relationship with the contact at the venue. It is, unfortunately, quite common for venues to sell their in house event organisers as wedding planners, and try to persuade your clients to not work with you any longer, as they will be able to provide the service themselves.

During the show round they need to see the whole venue, but try to make it personal by suggesting photos on the stairs, or point out a lovely spot in the garden, you can begin to bring their wedding day to life at the venue, which instils confidence that they've chosen the right person in you, and can help them choose a venue for their wedding day.

As well as setting the scene, they will want to know about the catering options, any suppliers you may choose or recommend that they work with. Many venues have restrictions on smoking, stiletto heels, candles, etc. You need to mention these to them, but have solutions (maybe not for the heels, but for smoking etc).

Whilst couples don't like hearing about weddings that you may have done before too frequently, if you can use different ideas, that you know work, and will give you more appeal, or that matches their ideas then do suggest them, as each time you show your interest and flexibility in their ideas and designs the more progress you will make.

Planning, Designing and Creating Weddings

12

12.1 Budgeting

Throughout the wedding planning process, you will need to keep an eye on how much they are spending. You can try to find out who is contributing from the family and whether they have paid or not, but it is not imperative, and unless you have a very good relationship with them, for some this may be too intrusive. As long as the couple have given you a figure to work with, then this is your figure to work to and you don't have to seek evidence that they can afford it.

When working out the budget, don't start putting in figures you know about and then work with what is left, as you could get too close to the wedding day and not have enough to pay for the remaining items.

Instead, you should calculate a budget for your clients at the very start, in your early sessions with them. You can do this by preparing a first draft of the budget and send it to them for their review. The best way to start is to create a budget spreadsheet, and insert all the suppliers and wedding items you know they are having, using average costs for suppliers that seem within their price range. When you have done this, you can send it to your clients and:

- Ask them to prioritise their most important suppliers/items
- Share with the bride and groom and get their approval (often worth showing them the least, middle and most expensive options)
- Add in contingency
- Clearly decide who will make the payments
- Draw up a payment plan. If the couple are saving through the duration of the planning then you will have to make sure that the payments aren't at the start of the planning stage, but mid way and towards the end. Most suppliers will look for an immediate deposit and the remainder around 6 weeks before the wedding day. You should make sure your own charges are well spread throughout the process.
- Don't forget to add in tips and VAT!

Courtesy of Alison and Steve Forrest, Elmcroft Studios, www.elmcroftstudios.com

Once they have reviewed this initial budget, you then need to have a discussion with them about which elements are your responsibility and which are theirs. For example:

- The wedding planner has a responsibility to ensure that the suppliers recommended are within the price range and are affordable
- The wedding planner has the responsibility to update the budget with costs known and confirmed
- The bride and groom have a responsibility to track their own additional expenditure towards the wedding or to provide this information to be included.

You should be wary of sharing the value of the wedding with anyone other than the bride and groom. Very often parents of the bride and groom don't know how much the total will come too, and are likely to have a heart attack if they did! Likewise, suppliers may ask what the total budget is, and they do not need to know. Ask yourself if you tell them – will it help them? Does knowing how much the couple have to spend help them to provide a quote? Arguably not if the requirements were clear, although letting them know how much is allocated to their particular item could help them price competitively if they really want to win the business.

As discussed earlier, in Chapter 6, you need to be clear on who will make the payments to the suppliers. Will it be the couple directly, or via you? If you are handling payments on their behalf, ensure that you factor in your banking charges, along with late payment charges (as these could potentially be your liability!)

12.2 Getting Started

The early stages of planning the wedding are very important. Not only is this when the key decisions are made, but also this is when your relationship with the couple is made. It is imperative that very early on you convince them that you are capable, committed and are open to their ideas and suggestions.

There is a lot of effort from you invested in the early stages. You need to make sure that you clearly understand your couple's ideas and requirements.

Things to consider are:

- Type of Marriage they want to have (both cultural, and also 'feel' of the day)
- Your involvement (are you helping with everything, or only selected suppliers)
- Size of wedding party (small and intimate or very big)
- Realistic Plans and Theme (how long until the wedding day, is it a 'traditional' wedding or a theatrical staged event)

Make sure that you understand and keep a record of the ideas and decisions that have already been made, so that you are not doing any work unnecessarily.

As discussed in Chapter 6, Suppliers, some couples want you to recommend suppliers that they know you have used before, others want those that they have met at wedding shows and others know people that they don't want! This can be because their friends used them, or that they don't like the supplier's style.

We have already discussed your approach to recommending suppliers. Will you just email over the website links and let them look for themselves, or write a short synopsis of each supplier, will you share the company name or keep it hidden? You may consider doing this if you are adding a mark up to the price – but this is both risky and also unlikely to work that well as very few people would choose suppliers without knowing the company name. Whilst they may trust you – they will also want to do their own research – after all it is their money!

Be prepared to have to search for new suppliers frequently. Throughout your planning process, always try to give them a choice of supplier. Even if they are only making a choice between 3 they will feel in control, and also they then take the responsibility for that choice, (and in your contract this responsibility is theirs and you have no liability for that choice, or non-performance of the chosen supplier).

For suppliers that are selling a specific service – like marquee hire or furniture hire then it is worth preparing all the quotes into one spreadsheet and then allowing the client to review the costs and items for hire/sale with the comparison. The more information that you can provide to help with the decision making the better, as normally this is a key reason you are hired. To save time with research and to recommend the most suitable companies.

Once the venue and caterers are chosen (including wedding location), then there is a general steady approach to the wedding day. Having discussed earlier on the approach you will take, you should remain consistent and recommend suppliers, wait for a choice (more research if necessary) and then confirm the booking with the supplier.

12.3 YOUR ROLE AS THE 'WEDDING PLANNER'

It is worth re-capping here, on your role as the wedding planner. Every single couple is different, and they'll all expect a different service and/or approach. In your initial conversation (especially before you agree a price), understand what you'll be expected to do. For example:

- Go to supplier meetings
- Call once a week for updates
- Meet with both mothers, the bride and bridesmaids
- Take them to dress fittings/food tasting/venue viewings
- Track expenditure
- Process each invoice and payment
- Be available at weekends/evenings
- Number of visits

Once you have an understanding of your role and what they want from you, you then can work out how long it will take you, depending on how you price, you can then set a price for your services.

It is worth now, going back to your business plan, and the work we've suggested that you do. With the learning you have done and information absorbed since you started this manual, take a look at your initial ideas for how you will price your services, and see if this is still your preferred approach, and take a look again at what level of detail you have considered. Did you think about the cost of venue visits (especially if you are offering 'packages'), banking charges for paying their suppliers, time spent attending meetings with the clients (and the cost of getting there).

Look at your literature you send through the eyes of your client. After receiving their contract, and agreeing the price would they be clear on how many meetings they have paid for, or whether you come to every single supplier meeting with them? Would they understand that they have a set number of meetings with you, or could they ask you to visit when they felt it would be a good time to catch up? Likewise, have you considered how much that will cost you as an overhead, if you went to see the client at their every request?

It is fine in the early months of your business to go to lots of meetings (and not be paid for it) as you want all the experience you can get, but hopefully as you become more and more busy, you may struggle to find the time to go to a 'meeting' that could have been dealt with over the 'phone or by email.

How will you share your ideas and ensure that you understand one another?

You will have so much contact with your clients over the planning period, that you will want to spend some time now, thinking about the main form of contact that you will have with your clients and, more importantly, how you will keep them updated on the progress of your wedding plans.

Spend some time now, thinking about how you will keep your clients updated on current budget expenditure, suppliers booked and those being researched, to those awaiting decision by the client. How will you keep track of outstanding actions, and things that need to be considered much later in the planning process?

Some suggestions for keeping track of wedding planning progress are:

- ✣ Have personalised pages on your website, which your client can sign in to, which shows progress against each of the activities that you have been commissioned to do. You may also want the client to be able to post/add comments on the website against recommendations and records that you have made.

    If you decide to adopt this approach, then make sure that you have the ability to update your website yourself, with a content management system, rather than rely on a website developer. As not only will this incur an expense, you are also at the mercy of their timescales rather than your own, and your updates may not happen as quickly as you would like.

- Provide the client with a folder, which has your branding on it, with tabs for each activity, and then print for them progress as it happens. This seems like a very good idea, and one which many clients will find appealing at the consultation stage, but realistically, it is a lot of effort on your behalf to print pages for the file, and also an expense for you. Also, you would have to decide what was printed and what wasn't. Over the course of a 12 month period you will send each other literally hundreds of emails, and printing all of those as a record of discussion is expensive, time consuming and will make searching for information very difficult, as you will only need the latest version, with an audit trail for discrepancies.

- Create a document that has activities listed in it, similar to those that you have agreed to provide the client in your service. You may wish to provide greater detail against each activity, which shows progress against the item. For example, rather than have Source and Book photographer, you may choose to record:

  - Recommend three photographers
  - Liaise with chosen photographer and agree price and contract
  - Pay deposit
  - Discuss requirements and confirm wedding day details
  - Final payment
  - Pre-Wedding final discussion

Then, against each activity you would record the **latest** status, and any actions for yourself or the client. A sample may look like this:

Activity	Status	Actions
Recommend 3 photographers	Document sent on the 25/08/09 by email for your review	Please review and provide your thoughts
Liaise with chosen photographer and agree final price and contract	Not started	This will be done following your choice of photographer
Pay deposit	Amount will vary on choice of photographer, but will be due on contract signature.	
Discuss requirements and confirm wedding day details		
Final Payment		Likely to be due 3 weeks before: **20/08/10**

With these thoughts in mind, take a look over your business plan, and review how you would work with your clients, and how you will communicate progress and keep them updated on your progress. It is worth trying to think of the quickest, easiest and most cost effective method.

The format that you choose should help you, where possible, to document agreements and instructions from your clients. You will also want to consider creating templates, so that you can re-use the documents and recommendations that you produce to save you time and to help you become familiar with the questions you want to ask and to find a mechanism that suits you.

Courtesy of Stephanie Mackrill Photography,
www.stephaniemackrill.com

Writing some fact sheets or hints and tips documents are a good time investment as you can use them over and over again. When you first take on a client they are very eager to get started, and you need to try to keep up with their desire to 'get going', which is very difficult because in the earlier stages of planning a wedding, it is the activities that take some time – such as looking for venues and choosing key suppliers such as caterers.

By being able to share information often – to give the couple something to read and consider – such as fact sheets, you can keep them informed and happy at little effort to yourself (as you'll be busy looking for suppliers).

Likewise, in the early stages of your business, invest lots of time in creating templates for things like recommended suppliers, colour ideas, table name ideas, how to do a table plan, wedding insurance comparisons, etc. This is information you will have to use time and time again, and it is good to create the fact sheets so that you learn at the same time, but also so you have information at your finger tips that you can share with your clients, when appropriate.

Quite often clients do change their minds – whether it be on how much they are looking to spend (so you have to be good at keeping track of expenditure) or if they 'start too fast' and go buying dresses, bridesmaid dresses and colour scheme things such as decorations, then they normally get replaced as their planning develops and their ideas grow.

Some other things to look out for that could cause you problems are:

- ✤ 'Falling in love' with items they just can't afford (normally a dress)
- ✤ Guest numbers increasing
- ✤ Theme taking over and needing to buy new items!
- ✤ VAT in addition to the price on the quote
- ✤ Not being able to get discounts
- ✤ Supplements on Menu dishes

- Not pricing for Jabs (vaccinations for honeymoon)
- Donation for the Church (not really optional!)
- Wedding party members (friends or family) becoming involved and pressurising the couple to try new ideas, and source new suppliers not previously on the budget (such as doves/chocolate fountain/chair covers/church flowers)

12.4 WORKING TOGETHER

Prepare a checklist of the key elements of a wedding day to use during the initial meetings you have with your clients to capture their requirements and then test these with the Bride and Groom to ensure you have captured them accurately.

The proposal document or/and your contract should really detail the activities that you are going to undertake. As already discussed you will want to pay particular attention to number of meetings with the bride and/or suppliers and your accessibility to the bride.

Once this has been documented and agreed as part of the contract then you must ensure that you use this document to manage the work you will do. Try not deviate, as the additional work that you undertake will become accepted as you just delivering the existing contract with no opportunity to seek additional payment. You may decide on occasion to do more than was requested, which is fine, if you have made a conscious decision to do so – not because you were forced to do so.

In the very early stages of planning the wedding, you will arrange to meet with the bride and groom in order to understand their vision for the day, themes, colours, what is important to them, what role they want to have in the planning of their wedding, any constraints and, of course, their budget.

Where the customer requirements change then the change needs to be assessed and priced and submitted to the bride for approval before the additional work is undertaken. Once agreed with the bride the contract can then be formally amended.

This is of course in an ideal world, you may feel the need to 'just let some things go', but do be prepared for the changes in requirements and what you will do to ensure that you are paid for any additional work that you undertake if you have not quoted for it and, therefore, won't be paid to do it.

Communication with the client is key to ensuring a successful wedding. However it is essential that the type and method of communications are clearly defined in the contract. (such as weekly telephone calls, emails, written report once a month).

You also need to give thought to Customer Satisfaction - How will you ensure that your customers are happy with the work that you are doing? You can tell yourself to look out for some key indicators:

- ✣ Are they chasing you for information
- ✣ Is their Mum suddenly involved in the meetings
- ✣ Are they asking you about cancellation process
- ✣ Do they say 'thank you' often?
- ✣ Do they seem relaxed or very stressed
- ✣ Do they say that they are finding it overwhelming, or that they feel out of control?

When they get stressed, nervous or irritable it could be the wedding nerves taking hold. You will need to ensure that you acknowledge that and ask what it is you can do to help?

Designing the Day

At the start of the wedding planning, the couple's expectations are very high, and they want you to show them how the whole day will look.

This can be difficult because you may not have found a venue yet, and they may not have decided on a style or theme.

You'll need to consider how you manage that early stage, as you don't want to have to re-do work at a later date, if the couple change their mind.

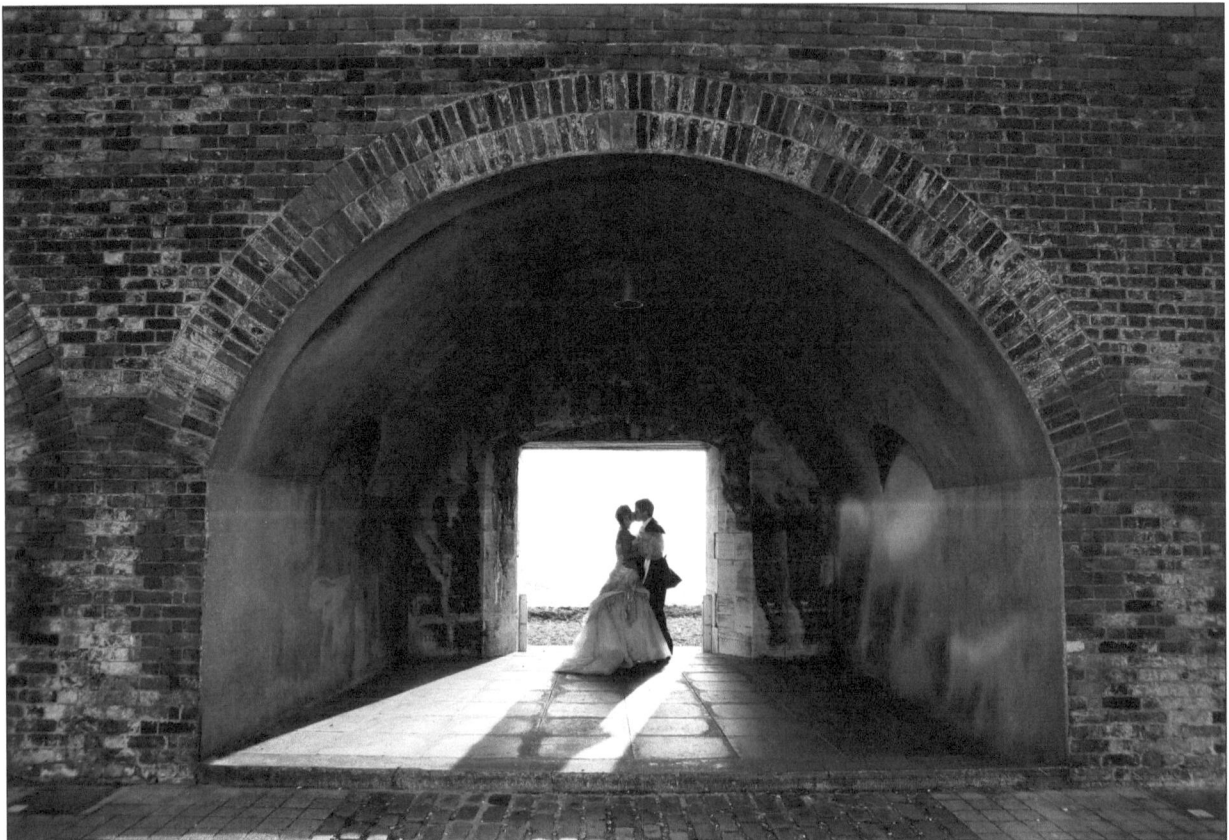

Courtesy of Danni Beach Photography
www.dannibeachphotography.com

How to be a Wedding Planner

Mood Boards

If the couple have some ideas, you can spend time creating mood boards. These can show various ideas and styles that will give them some decisions. Treat rejection as a positive statement – they don't like it – that's good – you can move on and suggest something different.

It can be a good idea to ask your clients to think about creating some Mood boards. Not only will it keep them occupied in the early stage, it prevents them from making rash decisions in a desire to just 'get going'. Likewise, it helps them see a bigger picture on how their wedding day will look and start to get a feel for the colour schemes that are in their mind.

Lastly, mood boards are also a way for the Groom (if not particularly involved) to get a feel for what the day will look like, they tend to be more visual people and, therefore, can see what they like or don't like, but wouldn't respond if you were just explaining a look to them.

Creating Themes

Themes can range from a very obvious theme that could include fancy dress, so, for instance, a medieval theme through to just using a subtle colour throughout the day. You'll get a feel for themes and be brimming with ideas after you have started to do a lot of research. One of the best places to do research, and to have an idea of current and future trends, is to keep an eye on wedding websites, and look at featured or real life weddings. Also read the message boards where future brides talk about their plans and swap ideas. This will give you an insight into the ideas and trends for the coming years.

> 'I soon learnt not to share all my ideas in the initial consultation, whilst its important to let them see that you have some good ideas, you don't want to give them lots of ideas because either they would then not book you and keep your ideas, or book you and then say that you haven't come with anything new!'
> Experienced Wedding Planner

Themes really are to give you some structure, to help aid in recommendations, choice and decisions made by the couple. Themes shouldn't overpower the day, or the planning, or otherwise every time the bride sees anything with a star/butterfly/colour on it she'll buy it, and you'll have a very difficult time getting it all out on the wedding day and not knowing where to put it all! Also, the more you have can dilute an effect and you end up with very little, just a lot of 'things'.

Once you have an idea of the style of the day, you may then want to encourage your clients to choose a main base colour and they can do this from looking at a colour wheel – or some paint magazines available from DIY shops – they show ranges of colours.

Courtesy of JoAnne Dunn Photography
www.joannedunn.it

Most people are always drawn to a colour, if you look around their home you may see a colour that is suitable and that they obviously like. Choosing a colour scheme is quite difficult for some weddings and easy for another. Some people like to start with the venue and work from there, others may like to look at colours that will suit themselves or their bridesmaids and use that as their basis for a colour scheme.

Colour Wheel

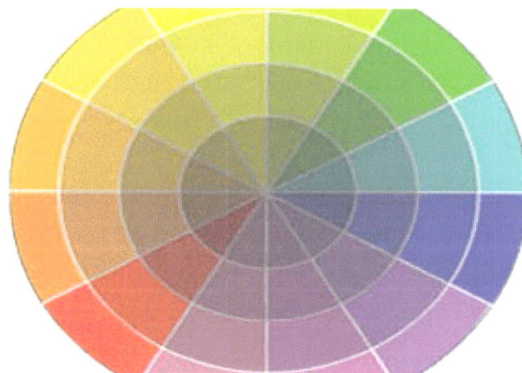

Once the main colour has been chosen, the colour wheel will show what other colours will go with this colour and decide whether to go for:

One Colour - could be determined by the colour of the bridesmaids' dresses, or even the main colour of the ceremony room. For example, if the bridesmaids were wearing violet coloured dresses, the flowers would be a variety of violet coloured flowers such as pansies and violets.

Opposite colours – this is when you would recommend that they chose colours which are opposite each other on the colour wheel. If the bridesmaids are wearing yellow, the flowers should be violet; yellow and violet are opposite each other on the colour wheel. If the colour of their dresses is a light shade, the complementary shade should be light, and darker shaded flowers should complement darker shaded dresses.

Three Colours - a colour triad is made up of three colours that are the same distance apart on the colour wheel, for example, green, violet and orange. You could either suggest that the bouquet is made up of three different colours, one being the colour of the bridesmaids dresses, or two colours with the colour of the bridesmaids' dresses being the third colour.

Two Colours Next to Each Other - this colour scheme involves using shades which are next to each other within the colour wheel, for example, green/yellow, green and blue/green.

Suggest to them to look into their garden (or a well looked after garden) in the season they are marrying in, if you have the opportunity and look at natural colours. It is very rare that a flower with more than one colour on it, doesn't look nice and complement itself.

Seasonal colours – you can suggest as a starting point that they consider seasonal shades for their wedding, to create a seasonal atmosphere.

  ✤ Spring - yellow, lilac, blue and white
  ✤ Summer - yellow, orange, red, pink, gold, hazy purple and green
  ✤ Autumn - yellow, orange, red, gold, brown, russet (reddish-brown) and cream
  ✤ Winter - strong dark red, russet, green, orange, gold, silver and white

If your client is still struggling, then it's worth asking a good florist to take them to a flower market and look at flowers and colours that attract them. Likewise, suggest that they get their 'colours' done. This will tell them whether they're a warm colour etc.

Courtesy of Stephanie Mackrill Photography – www.stephaniemackrill.com

The Venue will often dictate not only the theme of the day, but also the style of the wedding. A wedding that takes place in winter in a Stately Home, with the reception hosted in an antique style with dark wooden furniture and paintings on the wall, would not lend itself to a wedding where the bride and groom wore doc martins with totally funky hairstyles and a rock band. Equally, a football club location wouldn't suit a wedding where the relatives and guests were elderly, wore hats and were expecting a high quality, 6 course silver served meal overlooking a driveway and magnificent firework display.

The personality of the Bride, Groom, their chosen wedding party and families will also have a big say in the style of the wedding. If they are shy, then they won't feel comfortable in a very formal wedding reception, they are more likely to prefer a reception that has no top table, relaxed food service and reportage photographer that doesn't take group shots.

The budget, of course, plays a big part, but it shouldn't determine the style and theme of the day. This should be their personalities, theme ideas and expectations.

Lead up to the Wedding Day 13

Once the venue and caterers are chosen (including wedding location), then there is a general steady approach to the wedding day. Having discussed earlier in this book your preferred way of working with your clients, you should remain consistent and recommend suppliers, wait for a choice (more research if necessary) and then confirm the booking with supplier. Ensure all payments are made within the required timescales, whether this is by you or the client directly.

Then you record and track progress through to the wedding day. The next section of the manual focuses on the few weeks before the wedding and the day itself.

13.2 Preparing for the wedding day

If you are meeting with a client who is looking to book you to offer support and assistance on the wedding day itself, rather than ask for assistance in the planning, then this part of the book will be the most useful to you when planning how you will work with this client/service. The common term for a service offered where you are there for the wedding day only is 'Wedding Day Co-ordination'.

Regardless of whether you are just getting involved at this point (after the planning but before the day) or have had involvement through the whole of the planning process, you are likely to be asked during your meeting with the bride and groom on their wedding day timings.

You will need to be able to advise them:

   ✢   How long their service is likely to last
   ✢   How long in advance do they need to be there
   ✢   Can they really be late?
   ✢   What happens if they are late?
   ✢   How long will it take to get from the Church to the Reception?
   ✢   What time should the hairdresser be booked for?
   ✢   What time should the Groom get up (Yes we've had that one!)
   ✢   How long will it take for their nails to dry?

If you are going to meet with some clients who have planned the wedding themselves, then you will be new to the wedding arrangements.

It is wise to undertake a little research before you go to meet them and ensure that you understand where the wedding venue is, if it is easy to find and commute to and what the arrangements for the day are (Civil Wedding, Church Wedding, Formal Reception etc.).

In all cases, around 6 weeks before the wedding day, the Bride (and Groom) tend to feel that they're 'almost there' and at that time they'll start to feel nervous and want to ensure that you are now very involved.

Should the couple not have booked you since the start of their plans, but specifically want you to come in towards the end, then regular contact is beneficial for a number of reasons:

- ❖ The client wants to ensure that you have not forgotten about their wedding
- ❖ You may be able to add on additional services to the package price – i.e. attend additional meetings, a venue visit with the client, attend the rehearsal.
- ❖ You are less likely to 'lose' the booking should they decide (usually persuaded by the venue) to cancel your services
- ❖ You can recommend your preferred suppliers (you may want to consider commission), regardless of whether you take commission or pass savings to your client, working with your preferred suppliers makes the wedding day run more smoothly, reduces your workload

13.2 PRE-WEDDING MEETING FOR 'ON THE DAY' SERVICE

This section is written with the view that the couple have booked you for the wedding day coordination – rather than you being there throughout the planning process. This is a very popular package that many wedding planners provide.

Once you have arranged the pre-wedding meeting, its good practice to confirm the meeting time by email/letter. In this letter you should advise them that the meeting is likely to be an hour and half to two hours long, and at this meeting you will be asking the bride and groom to talk through their arrangements for the day, and ask them to provide you with information in order to prepare a timetable and ensure that their wedding day runs smoothly with their plans (again only if you're just starting to work with them – otherwise you would be taking all the information with you).

It is advisable to ask them in advance to collate all their supplier information and you could ask them to complete a template that you have created or just write down the details when you are there.

When you arrive at the client's home or agreed location for the meeting – it is a good idea to hold it at the venue if possible. If you do agree to meet at the venue, then telephone their contact there before hand, ask to arrive slightly earlier to meet the co-ordinator and ask if their wedding reception (and ceremony) room would be available to view.

Each time you go to a meeting you'll have different information available to you about the clients' wedding day. Some couples send lots of information about their day in advance, others expect you to be able to know what questions to ask and be able to pull it together into an understandable timetable. In your early days you may want a ticklist or list of questions, so that you can ensure you don't miss anything.

To get the meeting started, it is easiest to ask the client to talk you through the theme and feel of their day, and ask them to tell you what is the most important thing about their day to them. Everyone has different answers, it could be that they want it to run to time, or that everyone enjoys themselves, or that the room looks amazing.

Courtesy of JoAnne Dunn Photography
www.joannedunn.it

Then, throughout the meeting gradually guide them through the elements of their day. You are specifically interested in knowing the arrangements to ensure that there aren't double bookings in terms of timings, for example: The flowers being delivered to their home whilst they are at the hairdressers.

As you will experience, there are many things to consider. You will need to run through the arrangements in your mind as you discuss them and try to picture any potential hiccups.

You should also ask the client what they want you to do in the occurrence of a surprise – for example – the Groom/Bridesmaid/Mother has arranged a surprise for them – it could be pictures of them as children to be put up on the wall, different name cards or additional table decorations. It is worth being very clear in understanding what 'surprises' they would be happy with, and which they certainly wouldn't. Generally, anything which will embarrass the bride should be avoided, but it is best to ask, and even agree that you will tell the bride all 'secrets'. She then can make a decision on whether you go ahead or not, and then pretend to act surprised when the 'surprise' happens. This may ruin a surprise, but is a lot better than the worst case scenario which would be the Bride/Groom very disappointed and feeling that the look they had created had been ruined.

At the end of the meeting, you could run through any actions you've taken at the meeting and anything that they have said that they will do. Once back in your office, you can begin to create the wedding day timetable, and confirm arrangements with the suppliers, as well as carry out any actions that you took, reporting progress back to your clients.

The wedding day timetable is a very important document. When completed it will contain all the actions that you will need to carry out on the wedding day, it will also detail arrangements of all suppliers and any specific activities that the wedding party will need to carry out.

Courtesy of Alison and Steve Forrest, Elmcroft Studios. www.elmcroftstudios.com

The timetable is a business document and is limited to the activities you are responsible for ensuring happens and also times of arrival of wedding party, the ceremony etc.

When creating a wedding timetable, it is advisable to start in the middle of the timetable with the wedding ceremony and then work backwards. Once you've done pre-wedding then do after wedding. You will need to pay particular attention to the following:

Hair and make up arrangements – how many people will be having hair and make up done? How many staff will be in attendance? It is advisable for the bride to not be done last. (Although if they are starting early, not to do the bride first). Speak to the people performing the activities and ask them for their estimated times and how they are hoping to approach it.

Delivery of flowers. Which are going to the Bride, Church, Reception and Groom? Are they all separate deliveries or will you have to do some deliveries? Most people do not consider the Groom's flowers delivery – or do not have a specific delivery time for their flower delivery and have not considered that they may not be in when a delivery arrives.

Arrival times of suppliers and availability of the room. Arrival times of evening suppliers and times of the evening reception. It is worth exploring the opportunity to ask DJs and Bands to arrive prior to the wedding breakfast, otherwise there is no time or privacy for sound checks to take place.

Number of guests and table decorations – you need to allow a lot of time for table set up. Approximately allow a minute and half per chair cover and sash, and at least a half hour for name cards, if you have previously sorted them by table.

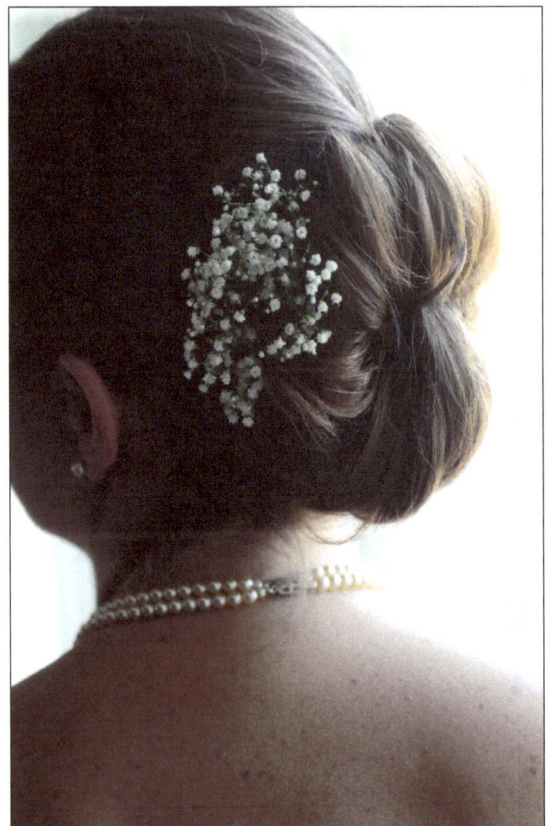

Courtesy of Stephanie Mackrill Photography – www.stephaniemackrill.com

Courtesy of Alison and Steve Forrest, Elmcroft Studios – www.elmcroftstudios.com

Going into dinner: Include the time that guests will be asked to take their seat and allow a lot of time for receiving lines if you are having one.

Also include an entry for the Introduction of the Bride and Groom, and name of the person making announcements, so that they can have a copy of the timetable to help as a prompt throughout the day.

Speeches – you can have just one entry 'Speeches' but do leave a generous time allowance. (They're very optimistic with 30 mins). It is worth writing in the text of the person making the announcement so they don't accidentally do it wrong, and also remind each speech maker of the person whom they should toast.

Your arrival and departure time – it is recommended that you don't consider leaving until the evening is underway. Be generous with your time in the morning of the wedding as you will always have unexpected tasks crop up. You will need to ensure that you consider travel time, parking and contingency times in your timetable.

It is also worth putting the contact phone number of each supplier against the suppliers name in your timetable, so that on the wedding day you have the information immediately to hand.

On completion of the timetable, it should be sent to the Bride and Groom for their review and approval.

You will then need to start to contact the suppliers and confirm the final arrangements with them. It is important to remember that the timetable is a guide, it is not your position to dictate to a supplier what time they should arrive, or finish. Instead, it is worth positioning with the supplier that you are checking that you have estimated their arrangements correctly following your meeting with your clients. It will start your relationship off on the wrong foot if they feel that you are telling them how to do their job.

You should always contact the venue and introduce yourself to the clients' contact, and also speak to the head waiter/banqueting manager/duty manager who will be working that day. Without this person's support your day will be a complete nightmare.

Wedding Day Timetable
Civil Wedding in Hotel
Couples Name and Name

Wedding Date

Time	Who	Location	Task
	Wedding Planner	Reception Location	Deliver to the hotel: Cake Table Names Name cards Table Plan & Easel Tea lights and coloured tea light holders Garden lights/candles/games Cash to pay suppliers (put in hotel's safe) Gifts for wedding party Notes for Usher for announcement
10.00	Make Up artist (mobile number)	Bride's room	Make up for: Bride, Bridesmaid 1, Bridesmaid 2, Bridesmaid 3 Mother of the bride
11.00	Wedding Planner		Walk through of ceremony with Bride & Bridesmaids test out cd player and music tie ribbon round scrolls chair covers and tie bows signs in car park
12.00	Hairdresser (mobile number)	Bride's room	Hair for: Bridesmaid 1, Bridesmaid 2, Bridesmaid 3, Bride
12.00	Groom & Party	Reception Venue	Arrives and checks in to Bridal Suite.
1.00pm	Florist (mobile number)	Reception Venue	Deliver flowers - Bouquets & Buttonholes - Table decorations
2.15pm	Photographer (mobile number)	Bride's room	Arrives and begins with 'getting ready shots'
2.15pm	Videographer (mobile number)	Bride's room	Arrives and begins with 'getting ready shots'
2.30pm	Groom & Party/Wedding Planner		Fix buttonholes
2.30pm	Ushers	Car park/Hotel entrance	Welcome guests and invite through to bar

Time	Who	Location	Task
3.00pm	Wedding Planner	Garden/Bar	Handout buttonholes to guests
3.15pm	Photographer	Garden/Bar	Photos of Groom & Party & guests
3.30pm	Wedding Planner	Ceremony Room	Check over & put on background music
3.30pm	Registrar		Meet Groom and confirm details
3.45pm	Best Man		Ask Guests to take their seats in the ceremony
3.45pm	Videographer	Ceremony Room	Set up in Ceremony room
3.50pm	Ushers	Ceremony Room	Accompany Grandparents and Parents to their seats
3.50pm	Ushers	Ceremony Room	Welcome guests into room and ask them to take their seats
3.55pm	Best Man	Bar/Gardens	Encourage remaining guests to take their seats
3.55pm	Registrar		Meet Bride and confirm details

Wedding Ceremony

Time	Who	Location	Task
4.00pm	Hotel		Serve Champagne and Pimms
4.30pm	Hotel		Begin to set up for the wedding breakfast
4.35pm	Photographer/Videographer	Garden/Bar	Shots of guests in garden
4.45pm	Wedding Planner	Reception	Put out: - Table centres - Table names - Name cards - 8x Candles & light them - favours - menus
5.00pm	Wedding Planner	Reception room	Turn on background music
4.50pm	Photographer	Gardens/Bar	Formal Group Shots
5.20pm	Best Man	Gardens/rooms	Make announcement for Guests to go into dinner
5.30pm	Bride & Groom		Announcement & welcome into dinner.
5.30pm	Guests	Reception room	Dinner is served
5.45pm	Wedding Planner	Gardens	Arrange meal for videographer/Photographer/Wedding Planner Short break
6.30pm	Wedding Planner	Garden	Put out garden Lighting/Decorations (luminaries)
7.00pm	Top Table		Speeches begin
7.30pm	Best Man		Ask Guests to go into bar for Tea, Coffee & 'Cutting of the Cake' (reminder: top up wine glasses & take with them)
7.00pm			Speeches
7.30pm	Guests	Reception Barn	Meal finishes

Time	Who	Location	Task
7.30pm	Wedding Planner	Reception Room	Prepare for evening reception
	Hotel		Remove some tables (Hotel)
			Change clothes where necessary (Hotel)
			Set up buffet table (Hotel)
			Replenish table tea lights and candles & light them (Wed. Plan)
			Collect up all table names and memorabilia and put in Bridal Suite (Wed. Plan)
			Move extra table decorations to other locations (Wed. Plan.)
			Collect not taken wine and put into your Bar area
			two vases of sunflowers on the top table – keep them separate not use them again in the evening
7.45pm	Bride & Groom		Cake & coffee with guests in lounge
7.45pm	DJ	Dancefloor	Arrives and Begin to play
8.00pm	Bar	Bar	Bar will open, free for £1000
8.00pm	Ushers	Car Park, Courtyard, Reception Bar	Welcome newly arriving guests
8.00pm	Evening Guests	Car Park	Guests begin to arrive
8.30pm	Bride and Groom	Dance floor	First dance
9.00pm	Photographer		Leave
9.00pm	Videographer		Leave
9.00pm	Wedding Planner		Leave.
10.00pm	Hotel	Buffet Table	Serve evening buffet
12.00am	Everyone		Evening Finishes

NOTES:

+ Hair and Make Up
+ Reception set up
+ Ceremony set up
+ Deliveries by suppliers
+ Hotel Check in
+ Supplier Management

As mentioned in the previous pages, you should ensure that you have clearly thought about all of these activities and planned them into your timetable accordingly. Hair and Make up timings need careful arrangement. You should 'timetable' who goes when. Put the bride in the middle, and generally, make up is always done after the hairstyle. Always ensure she has a top on that un-does (like a shirt) rather than a t-shirt that has to be taken off over her head.

In preparation for the wedding day, you may need to arrange a time to collect all the items for the wedding from the Bride/Groom – or arrange where to collect them from – i.e. they may take them to the venue.

It is quite common for a wedding planner to take the Bride/Groom's or both of their overnight bags to their hotel rooms for their wedding night. Some hotels won't let you go to their room, so make sure that you check that their bags have been taken to their room before they go up there.

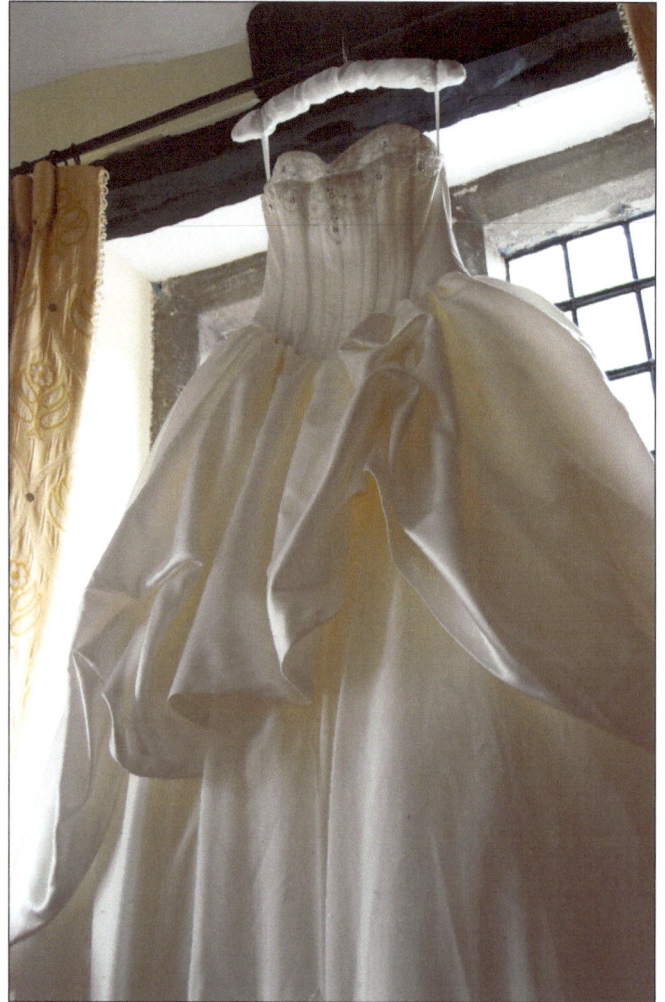

Courtesy of Alison and Steve Forrest, Elmcroft Studios – www.elmcroftstudios.com

Wedding Set Up 14

14.1 CEREMONY SET UP

If the wedding is at the same venue as the reception (i.e. it is a civil wedding) then you may be using the same chairs and flowers, and possibly even the same room. If you are using the same room, then the set up for the wedding breakfast can only be done after the ceremony takes place, and therefore deliveries of cakes are not useful until after the ceremony.

Setting up the Civil Ceremony room is normally done by the venue staff – however, in venues such as barns, it may be your responsibility to lay out the chairs and get the room ready, but there should be a representative from the venue there and they will normally give this aspect their most attention as they want to ensure that the Registrar is happy with proceedings.

Typical items at a ceremony that you will oversee are:

Aisle runners. This is a length of fabric that is laid down the aisle between the chairs to create an aisle, or to cover tired carpet. It can be ordered in the clients' colours and often can be personalised. If you are ordering one, do check the width of the aisle first, and also check with the Chuch/venue that they will allow it, as some places do not allow them for health and safety reasons.

Pew Ends – whilst typically used in a church, pew ends can be ordered to hang on the end of the rows of chairs. They are going to be slightly different to Church pew ends – such as loops of a flower rather than flowers put into an oasis.

Confetti – normally fresh petals, will be your responsibility to prepare and have ready to be handed out after the ceremony. This could be the role of the bridesmaids, but often wedding planners are also asked to do it.

Ensure that the **Order of Services** are available, and have them handy to give to the Ushers. Take them out of the boxes and store the boxes somewhere easy to get to but out of sight, so that you can use them after the ceremony to collect up any that are left behind. Try to keep at least one for the couple as a keepsake.

Make sure that any **music** needed is at the cd player and that you test it prior to people arriving. You will need to make sure that guests can hear it and so can the bride who will be waiting outside for her 'cue'.

If they are having **singers** (such as a Gospel choir) make sure that there's water and glasses available for them (not necessary in a Church).

Same for any **musicians** – such as harpist, violinist etc. Make sure that they have enough room to move, and be able to play. Also be aware that if there are number restrictions in the room for the ceremony, then you need to count all suppliers within these numbers.

Put out any **'reserved'** cards in the front rows for immediate family and bridesmaids. This isn't a necessity but can be helpful if you need to keep a number of seats free.

Ensure that **readings** are at the place where they will be read prior to the ceremony starting so that the readers' job is easier to do. This can be on a lectern, or just the print out is at their seat.

Ring Cushions aren't that popular, but some people do use them. You should consider how you will secure the rings to ensure that they don't fall off as they are taken up the aisle. In this picture there are pins used to keep them in place. The ribbon is looped into the ring, then a pin is placed in the ribbon to keep the ring secure. Without the pin, the rings slide across the pillow, and are likely to be dropped as a young child carries them up the aisle.

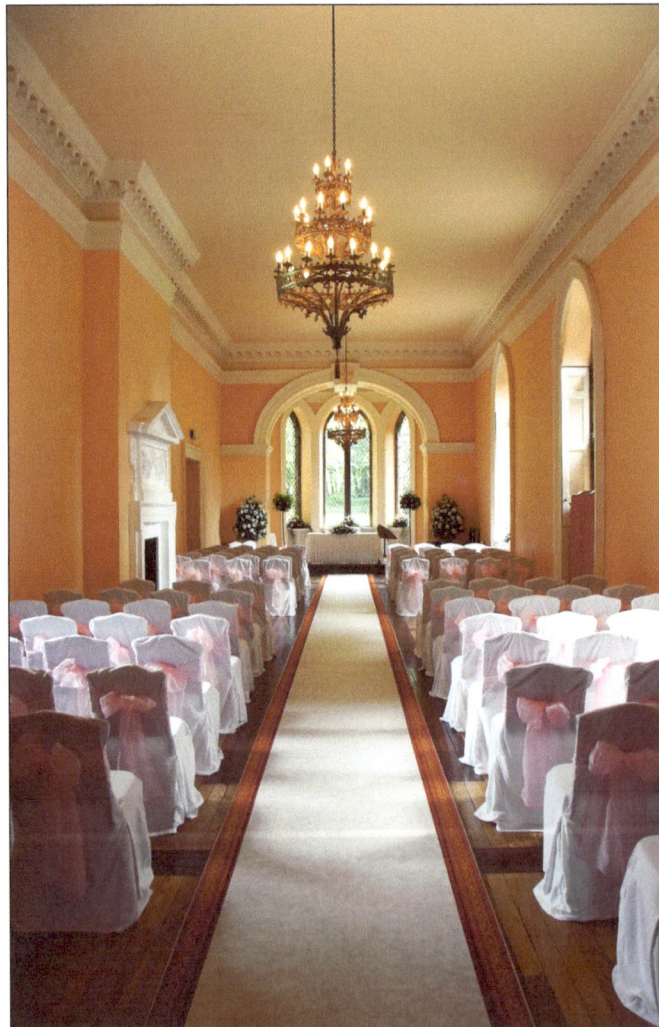

Courtesy of Alison and Steve Forrest, Elmcroft Studios – www.elmcroftstudios.com

The Ceremony

If the wedding is a civil one, it is worthwhile in introducing yourself to the Registrar when they arrive. If you are responsible for playing the music (on a cd player) during the service, then the Registrar will talk you through when to play it before the ceremony starts. They will normally look at you and nod when appropriate during the ceremony to inform you when to play and stop the music. The Registrar will also want to make sure that there is nothing planned for the ceremony that she/he has not already agreed to (i.e. change of music).

You should encourage the Groom, Best Man and Ushers to arrive approximately 45 to 30 minutes prior to the service beginning. You should definitely greet the Groom if you haven't seen him already and just have a quick chat. Ask the Groom how he's feeling and if the ceremony and reception are in the same place show him the reception room set up (if applicable), run through any issues that you have that you NEED him to know – it really is a need to know basis, they haven't hired you to know of situations or issues that are irrelevant or likely to stress them out unnecessarily.

Introduce yourself to the Best Man and Ushers. You will need to use your judgement as to whether the Groom wants to talk to you to ease his nerves or just wants to be left alone. The Groom will need to spend sometime with the Registrar to confirm his personal details and that he is who he has said that he is. In a Church he'll speak to the Minister/Vicar/Priest who is performing the marriage.

You'll also need to show the Ushers where the Orders of Service are and just brief them on whether it is one between two or one each. Also remind them of any special requests – such as reserved seating for immediate family or old relatives. Remind them also that its Bride's family on the left and Groom's on the right.

When the photographer arrives, have a quick chat with them – see how it's gone so far, advise them of any issues, locations of things if needed such as confetti so that they can take pre-used shots. (Photographs like this are good for your portfolio)

Hopefully the Bride and Groom will have chosen hymns for the service that everyone knows. There's nothing worse than a church with no-one singing. Don't try to sing up unless a) you know the song and b) you can sing! When you work with a couple to choose their music, you may want to recommend they think about 'school assembly' songs. In other words, the ones that most people will remember singing at school.

You may have it as your responsibility to ensure that you pay the organist, bell ringers, Choir and make a donation to the Church. Try to do it before the ceremony as afterwards you'll want to leave to get to the reception.

Encourage, where possible, guests with babies to sit near the back. You can have a quiet word with them before the ceremony starts to say that you can take the baby outside if it cries, if they wish, so that they can continue to watch the wedding. Some guests will take no notice of this, and sit at the front and let their baby cry. There's little you can do about this, as it is their choice.

Due to road works, accidents, public transport etc., there may always be people arriving late. They are going to feel bad enough when they arrive, so great them with a smile, have some Orders of Service in your hand, and then wave them in during a noisy bit – i.e. when asked to stand/sit, or a hymn and their entrance will be less noticed.

During high season there could easily be weddings before and after your wedding. Try to be efficient with the 'decorations' that you need to put out and collect at the end of the wedding. In a Registry Office you are likely to get 5 minutes maximum. It is becoming very popular to reserve seats for main wedding party guests and in a busy Registry Office this may be the most you can do. With weddings in Churches, in high season, there are likely to be more than one wedding, which means the flowers chosen will be chosen by the Church florist not the bride, to suit all the weddings that day, and can not be removed by you to take to the reception, unless previously agreed.

Once everyone in the ceremony room is ready and guests start to arrive, all that is left for you to do is to see the Bride and her bridesmaids. The Bride's mother traditionally is the last to enter the ceremony, before the bride and her father. It's a good idea to suggest to an Usher or the Best Man to walk her down the aisle to her seat.

When the Bride arrives, with her bridesmaids, catch her eye and say 'hi', and wish her luck or a similar pleasantry. Again, if she wants to talk let her – otherwise just stay out the way. As the Groom will have done, the Bride will need to speak with the Registrar/Vicar to confirm her name, address, date of birth to ensure that they are marrying the correct person.

It is at this point that you will have done everything that you can do and you'll take a back seat until the end of the service. It is advisable to have some Orders of Service in your hand for any late comers.

After the ceremony, the Bride and Groom will leave the room/Church first, followed by their parents, then bridesmaids and Ushers. Ensure that the Bridesmaids have the confetti to give out if applicable.

Depending on the location – such as Church, Registry Office or the same venue, the guests will follow the Bride and Groom outside.

Look out for the Marriage Certificate which often the best man will have and suggest that you take it. If the Bride and Groom are staying on site arrange for it to go in their room. If you are travelling to a different location it may be wise to let him keep it until you're back at the venue.

Courtesy of Danni Beach Photography
www.dannibeachphotography.com

Assuming that the ceremony is at the same place at the reception, following the wedding the Bride and Groom will be swept away for photographs. If the ceremony is at an alternative location then photographs will still take place at the wedding location, but you should leave and go on to the reception venue. Often the photographer will take the couple to some locations along the route back, and stop for pictures, so do not worry if they do not arrive for some time.

Courtesy of Mike French, www.meonshoreweddings.co.uk

Reception Set Up

Normally you would begin setting up a wedding reception in the reception venue, assuming that the ceremony was in a different place, before the wedding ceremony. On arrival at the venue, ask to speak to the wedding co-ordinator/duty manager – the person whose contact details you would have had and would have contacted in the week leading up to the wedding. This is the most courteous approach, as then they know you are there, remind them who you are, and they can help you with issues if you have any.

When you begin to set up the reception, you really would need the tables and chairs to be already out so that you can begin your set up. There is a chance that the room wouldn't have been prepared, and if this is the case you will need to encourage the staff to get the room set up as soon as possible, as without the cloths on the tables you will not be able to put flowers on the tables when the florist arrives, or any of your name cards, confetti etc. on the tables. It is also advisable to call the florist and inform them of the delay if you think it will affect their delivery and set up. It's likely that they'll have other deliveries and therefore coming to you slightly later when the room is ready will mean that they will be able to ensure that they stay for the time necessary to be there.

There may be other tasks you can do if this occasion arises, such as chair covers on the chairs, or putting the couple's suitcases in their room, or having a walk round to familiarise yourself with the venue.

When the tables are in place and the cloths on, you can begin the set up. Firstly make sure that all additional tables are in place so when deliveries are made you can direct the supplier to the location of their product, for example – cake table.

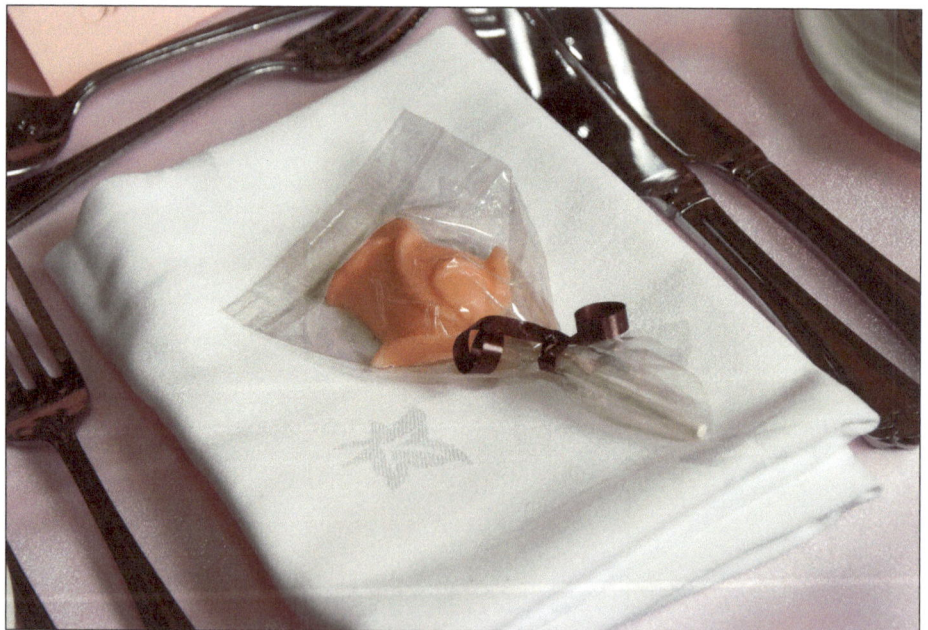

Courtesy of Alison and Steve Forrest, Elmcroft Studios – www.elmcroftstudios.com

Firstly you would put out the first layer of the table decoration – so for instance any organza table overlays. Then put out place cards as per the clients request (ensuring that you acknowledge 12 o'clock and 6 o'clock). Lay out favours and then any additional table decorations – tea lights (put the candles in and also put up the wick to make it easier when you have to light them), confetti, petals etc. When adding the last touches always work from the top table and then work downwards, that way if you run out the bride and groom are less likely to notice that the sprinklings are sparse at the back of the room!

Once the staff have laid out the cutlery, glasses and napkins, go back round the room and double check each setting, ensuring that no cutlery is missing or glasses are dirty. Also ensure that each place setting has a chair and highchairs are in the right place.

Whilst you are setting up the room, you're likely to get interrupted a lot and you will begin to feel that you are getting behind on your timings, which is why you need to add in some contingency time.

Do utilise the venue's staff if you think that it's within their remit – but remember that you want the client's day to be a success and, ultimately the venue to recommend you to other suppliers and clients, so try not to come across as bossy!

Your suppliers should also arrive throughout the morning when you are there, typical deliveries will include:

Flowers - these will be for the tables both centrepieces and possibly long and low for top table, displays for the front door or windowsills or toilets etc. Possibly bridal flowers if the bridal party are at the venue already (civil ceremony). If you do have the bridal flowers then you should ensure you deliver them to the wedding party and assist the men with attaching their buttonholes.

Cake - when it arrives ensure that it fits the description given to you by the client. Ask the delivery person to put it on the table provided and then take a photograph of it. If they do not put it on the table then take a photo of it as delivered. This is very important as there may be an accident before or after it arrived, and you will need the evidence to ascertain who's responsibility the damage is.

Casino – these are hired for the evening entertainment, they tend to need a big area, its risky to have it too far from the main evening reception, as you may find that a large proportion of the guests spend the evening there, rather than in amongst the rest of the guests with the band/disco etc.

Courtesy of JoAnne Dunn Photography
www.joannedunn.it

Chocolate Fountain – do not underestimate the space that a chocolate fountain needs and ensure that they have it. They often won't arrive until the evening.

DJ – sometimes the DJ will be asked to set up in the morning before the reception starts, as the client won't want them setting up when their guests are there, but normally the DJ sets up in the evening after the reception.

Crèche - If your wedding has a crèche ensure that they have the space and everything they need, but if things are missing, or they need additional equipment, where possible try to get them to go direct to the venue contact, as this will eat away at your time.

You will however, want to confirm their timings with your timetable. Especially with regards to photographs that their children need to be in and food times.

You will not see and possibly not speak to the Cars, Videographer or Photographer until later in the day.

When the room is all set up you may want to take a photo and text it to the Bride – only do this if you've asked him/her in advance if they'd like it, but it can be a good idea as the bride will never see the room looking perfect, she normally sees it when the guests are all sat down (especially if you have a civil ceremony with chair covers that you are texting a photograph of).

Courtesy of Alison and Steve Forrest, Elmcroft Studios – www.elmcroftstudios.com

It is also worth recommending to your client that they prepare their table decorations as follows:

Use a freezer bag or shoe box PER table, and put into it:

- ❖ favours per person (some people have individualised favours - in which case definitely do this)
- ❖ a list of the names of people on that table indicating who is at 12 o'clock (ie top table being 12 o'clock) and whether they want it to go clockwise/anticlockwise
- ❖ the table name cards for that table
- ❖ any table decorations – such as table name, additional decorations.
- ❖ Table confetti etc can just be kept in the one bag and then scattered last.

How to be a Wedding Planner

Simple activities such as the layout of the table cards can take so long. It is often difficult to share this task as you normally just have one copy of the table plan. If you do have a large number of guests, then ensure you have a couple of copies of the table plan, showing where everyone is sitting.

Common problems at Reception Venues include:

- Table centres need putting together
- Catering staff don't turn up until the latest moment – just as you need to have completed set up and leave for the Church
- More than one wedding and suppliers getting muddled
- Guests cancelling or confirming at last moment
- Restrictions on candles/naked flames
- Name cards being difficult to lay out
- No where to hang the table plan

Your timetable will not always match with some of your suppliers. For instance, your cake supplier may not need to deliver and set up the cake until an hour before the Bride and Groom and their guests enter the reception room. However, this could be 2 hours after you last left it.

If you haven't seen the cake being delivered (and approving it) then you will not be able to answer the bride's question should she ask. However, you have to make a decision on the most sensible time slot, and trust people's professionalism.

Equally it is very important that you see the delivery of the following before you leave the venue and go to the ceremony:

- Flowers
- Arrival of catering staff
- Meet the toastmaster/Venue manager/Catering manager
- Ask to be shown round the venue so that you know where the toilets for both ladies and gents are
- Cake
- Overnight bags
- Presents for the bridal party.

Other major questions you'll need to know answers to so that you can address any issues in advance are:

- Table plan – is there an easel and is it an easel or a flip chart? If a flip chart then consider the style of the wedding and your clients – will this be a problem or will they be ok with it?
- If you have been asked to fix items to the wall/outside/ceilings are you able to do so – and will you be able to do so?
- How they want their napkins tied/displayed – will the Hotel do this or will you have to?
- If there are chair covers advise the hotel of this and also ensure you call to confirm delivery.
- Whether there is a cake stand and knife for the client to use.
- Is parking going to be a problem (especially for you), what are the regulations, can you reserve a space, if its chargeable inform your client in advance so you can bill for the costs.

In the case of something going wrong, it is really your judgement call as to how you decide to rectify it. Something like a cake being dropped can be rectified by going to a local supermarket and buying their standard three tier cake, and use some ribbon and flowers to decorate it. Your key decision point would be to try and judge what the bride would feel, and whether she would prefer a cake at the wedding, even if it wasn't what she wanted. Or, if she can't have what she wanted then not to provide anything.

As you become more experienced you will be able to think and know of some 'back up plans', but it is worth thinking of some prior to a wedding day.

Courtesy of Alison and Steve Forrest, Elmcroft Studios – www.elmcroftstudios.com

The Reception

17.1 THE TOAST MASTER OR MASTER OF CEREMONIES

A Toastmaster is an experienced public speaker who will manage the manoeuvring of guests from place to place expertly, and because they are formally dressed and have loud, informative voices people will listen and obey.

The role that a toastmaster performs compared to your own is very different. The only places where you are likely to brush against one another is with their way of doing things and the bride's, but if you handle the conversation before hand and explain that your role is to oversee the whole day, and supplier deliveries etc, then they will be comfortable that you have different roles and your relationship will be fine. Do talk through your timetable with them before hand and be receptive to their recommendations and proposed changes.

Should your Bride and Groom ask a friend to be the Master of Ceremonies, then it is very helpful for that person if you provide them with a cut down version of the timetable providing key activities and when they need to speak. Add in the actual text that they need to say in advance. They don't need to stick to this rigidly, but it is a helpful prompt for them.

Generally, most friends performing this role are very professional and honoured to do so. Very occasionally, they may have one too many drinks and they begin to make announcements all the time, and just talk endlessly into a microphone. If you can't subtly ask them to be quiet, then it is best to ask the Best Man to have a word. They will be more respectful to the Best Man, and that conversation is best placed with him.

17.2 RECEIVING LINES

Receiving Lines take place so that the hosts of the Wedding and members of the Bridal Party can formally meet all the guests and welcome them to the wedding. There are pros and cons to this tradition. It can take a long time to welcome all of the guests into the reception, but the hosts can be assured that all guests have been welcomed personally, albeit briefly. It also gives the guest the opportunity to be able to thank the host for their invitation, and to speak to both the Bride and Groom.

The Receiving Line takes place as the guests enter the reception room, after the ceremony, photographs, welcome drinks and canapés. There are the standard receiving lines, which have been detailed here, but you can make some minor changes depending on their own personal family situation.

This receiving line starts with a member from each family. As guests arrive, one of them will be able to recognise the guest and can then introduce them to the other family. For example, the Bride's Mother can introduce a guest from her family to the Groom's family etc.

1   Bride's Mother
2. Groom's Father
3. Groom's Mother
4. Bride's Father
5. The Bride
6. The Groom
7. Chief Bridesmaid
8. Best Man

This next receiving line, is more popular as it looks more logical, but it does mean that the guests from the Groom's family are not introduced to the Bride's Mother and Father. However, many couples overcome this obstacle by asking their Master of Ceremonies or Wedding Co-ordinator to announce the name of each guest to the Bride's Mother who is the first in the line up.

1   Bride's Mother
2. Bride's Father
3. Groom's Mother
4. Groom's Father
5. The Bride
6. The Groom
7. Chief Bridesmaid
8. Best Man

The traditional Jewish receiving line is slightly different, but is a practical alternative if the previous two don't suit your needs, especially if you have a large bridal party. It also means that you will not need to choose one Bridesmaid to join the receiving line.

1   Bride's Mother
2. Bride's Father
3. The Bride
4. The Groom
5. Groom's Mother
6. Groom's Father

There are other alternatives that you can adopt at a wedding. If you feel that the couple have too many guests and are very restricted by time, then you could consider recommending that they have a much shorter receiving line such as the following:

1   Bride's Mother
2. Groom's Mother
3. The Bride
4. The Groom

How to be a Wedding Planner

It becomes more difficult, where parents may be divorced and do not wish to stand next to one another. In this scenario, modify any of the above versions to suit your clients' needs. A receiving line can be flexible and used to suit the parental relationships and number of guests that have been invited. If the couple have paid for the wedding costs themselves, then they may wish to welcome their guests by themselves.

17.3 WEDDING BREAKFAST

The wedding breakfast is the first meal served to the couple as Husband and Wife and is therefore called their 'Breakfast' but it is their reception.

After the wedding ceremony, you want to leave as soon as reasonably possible to get to the venue that the reception is being held at. This should be already set up with all the tables and the wedding decorations in place.

On arrival you'll need to let the event manager/head waiter know that the guests will shortly be arriving (especially in bad weather if they are likely to be early).

Your first task is to make sure that the welcome drinks are ready, and that the arrival area for the guests is clear, tidy and ready to receive the guests.

Run through the order of events with the head waiter/event manager and the Toastmaster if there is one.

- ✤ Will the speeches be before the meal?
- ✤ Do the Bride and Groom want to be announced?
- ✤ Are there presents to be distributed for the mothers, bridesmaids etc.
- ✤ Point out where key people are sitting, such as grandparents as they aren't likely to be at the top table.

A problem that you may face at a wedding (especially if the staffs are from an agency) is their standard of appearance. Be prepared to ask them to smarten up if you feel that the Bride and Groom (and more likely their parents) will notice and be unhappy – untucked shirts, laddered tights are normally seen to be unacceptable.

Have a walk round the room before the guests come in to make sure that the decorations (table centres, favours, chair covers, pictures etc) are all correct, tidy and that any candles or tea lights are lit.

Courtesy of Alison and Steve Forrest, Elmcroft Studios –
www.elmcroftstudios.com

Ensure that you point out to the waiting staff those people (their places) that have a special allergy or have a different meal. You could mark the back of their name card so that the waiters can easily see.

When the welcome drinks and canapés are being served, take a drink to both the Bride and Groom and ask if you can get them anything else. It's imperative that you do this, as it is very common for the couple not to be offered a drink during the photographs and have to watch everyone else enjoy a drink whilst they had their pictures taken. They will often want a glass of water too.

During the welcome drinks and photographs you will have other suppliers to co-ordinate, such as a string quartet or harpist, magician, doves etc. Any performing supplier should be encouraged to start when the guests arrive. They are entitled to breaks and often request food, but do try to prevent the food till the welcome drinks are over.

You will have discussed these issues in advance and agreed timings with the supplier, but again, a worse case scenario is that of the 2 hour playing time, they take a 30 minute break.

Before the guests take their seats for dinner, you should go into the room and re-check the table settings and other decorations, as well as start to light the candles. You should also introduce yourself to the Toastmaster if there is one. Otherwise speak to the person who is the 'MC' (Master of Ceremonies) to run through timings, and if they want you to let them know when you're ready for announcements. If this person is a member of the wedding party then you may want to prepare in advance some slips of paper which detail what to say and when.

If there is a receiving line, then try to put the table plan outside the room so that guests can study it whilst in the line, not after, which creates a further bottle neck.

When all the Guests have taken their seats, then the Bride and Groom are normally introduced to the room, such as " Ladies and Gentlemen, please be upstanding for the Bride and Groom – Mr and Mrs xxxxx!" there are alterations to this, but its relatively standard. (include this on your timetable with a named person – so that they too were aware and could ensure that they had prepared).

Be prepared to assist with the service of the champagne. This is one of the areas where you're likely to perform outside your role, but it is important to ensure that all guests have champagne before the toasts begin. This is a story likely to get back to the Bride or Groom.

Beforehand you should know when they want the cake to be cut, and then when and how to serve it. Such as on the evening buffet, with coffee or in cake boxes.

Ensure that you know what song the first dance will be. Check that the DJ has it. Let the DJ know that the first dance will soon happen, and ask the bride and groom whether you, the DJ or the MC/Toastmaster will announce them onto the dance floor.

At this time, you would normally take a break and go outside and have a snack provided for you to eat.

During the wedding breakfast you can prepare for your next activities, for example, if there are candles to go out after the reception for the evening you can put these in place now – typically they'd go in the gardens, driveway, any fireplaces etc.

How to be a Wedding Planner

You can also use this time to speak properly with the photographer and videographer and any other suppliers still at the wedding, who will also be taking their break. Very often suppliers will want to talk about you and your services, how much did the couple pay and what did you think about them. You should give prior thought to answering these questions. You should also use this time for networking, you ideally would like the photographer to give you some pictures they have taken of the wedding for your website/portfolio. Likewise some footage from the videographer will also be advantageous.

Evening entertainment may also arrive during the meal. If the evening reception is in the same room as the wedding breakfast then they shouldn't go in until the guests have come out (you would have discussed this with both your client and the supplier prior to the wedding). If the reception is in another room then you would show the suppliers where to go. Typical suppliers arriving are Bands, DJ, Dancers, Chocolate Fountain, Casino.

When the reception begins to come to an end you should make your presence known. Go to the Top Table and see the Bride and Groom and ask them how everything is going. If you have been asked to get gifts etc. ready for the speeches then you'd discuss this with the couple at this point. Do remember that gifts are normally a surprise so should be discreet (you may have wanted to put them somewhere near the top table during the room set up).

Sometimes you may be asked on the day or in the days prior, questions that you weren't expecting, a couple of which are below:

Some couples ask their bridal party to pay for their own outfits. As you are attending the wedding day, and it is likely to be the first time you have met many of the Bridal Party, you won't have had the opportunity to fend off this problem in advance.

Be prepared to be asked by any member of the Bridal Party (or their parents) if it is normal for the Bridesmaids and Ushers/Best Men to have to pay for their outfits themselves. Be cautious with your answer as you may not know what the couple's arrangement has been.

You may need (and are almost likely) to prompt people to do the tasks that they were asked to do. This can be really difficult, so be prepared to have to tackle this problem. Bridesmaids and the groom's men are just as popular on a wedding day as the Bride and Groom, as they may have been in contact with a lot of the guests when arranging stag

Courtesy of Alison and Steve Forrest, Elmcroft Studios – www.elmcroftstudios.com

and hen parties, surprises, the speeches and will probably be friends with a lot of the guests. It can be hard for them to 'get away' to carry out their tasks, so do be prepared to have to do it for them at times.

Speeches

18

First Speech
> By person who gave bride away
> Toasts the Bride and Groom

Second Speech
> By the Groom
> Toast the Bridesmaids

Third Speech
> By the Best Man
> Toasts the Bride and Groom

Speeches at weddings traditionally happen after the wedding breakfast. But, if you feel that the Groom, Best Man or Father is particularly nervous, you may recommend that they have the speeches before the meal. This then allows them to get it out of the way, relax and enjoy the meal and wine.

Assure them that very few people are practised public speakers, but if they practise, relax and are prepared it is unlikely to be a very unpleasant experience. The guests will be in good spirits through the day's celebrations and will laugh at the jokes and no doubt cry at the sentimental moments.

The speeches are not the most important part of the wedding, and if speaking publicly really is too hard, then ask someone else to take their place or minimise the Speech to include the toast only. Most speeches are typically 5 to 15 minutes.

The Wedding Co-ordinator, Hotel Event Manager, Toastmaster, Best Man or one of your guests should announce each speaker briefly. If speeches are after the meal, at the end of dessert each speaker is called in turn. The guests are expected to stand for the toasts, except for those being toasted, but this rarely happens, most people will toast from where they are seated.

First Toast

The first person to speak is traditionally the person who gave the Bride away. They will say a few words about the Bride and Groom, before proposing a toast to the health of the Bride and Groom.

Typically the following points are included in this speech:-

+ Opening – thanking everyone for attending, mention how well the   wedding has gone so far.
+ Stories about the Bride, watching her grow up, their hopes for her, how well she is doing and how beautiful she looks.
+ Welcome the Groom into the family, what they may have thought when they first met him.
+ Include the Mother of the Bride, especially if she's not speaking herself.
+ Finish with a toast to the Health and Happiness of the Bride and Groom.

REPLY TO FIRST TOAST

The Groom replies to the first toast on behalf of the Bride and himself. He then can give a short speech which should or could include:-

+ Thank the first speaker for their kind words and toast
+ Acknowledge his new family, and their welcome to him into their family.
+ Thank the guests for coming and for their generosity with their gifts
+ If they have gifts, now is the point to hand them out. Keep it brief and suggest they are given to the most important people – i.e. Mothers, Bridesmaids, Best Man and Usher.

SECOND TOAST

The Groom then toasts the Bridesmaids.

Some brides, whose father is not present, choose to say a few words of their own. They can either say this speech first or after the Groom has spoken. This speech is entirely flexible, here are some ideas to include:-

+ Thank everyone for attending, choosing to mention especially those friends you have helped her at a particular point in her life or who have provided support through the wedding planning, or those that have travelled far.
+ Thank those people who have helped and supported her during the planning of her wedding.
+ Include some special words about her parents, especially her Mum, not only in her help with the run up to the wedding, but to thank her for her help over the years.
+ She could also echo her husband's speech, including how they met, or how he proposed and how pleased she is to be his wife.
+ A new American idea is for the Bride to finish with a toast to the guests.

Reply to Second Toast

The best man replies to the second toast on behalf of the Bridesmaids, and then makes his speech in which he talks about the Groom and reads out any messages or telegrams.

The Best Man's speech is usually the most entertaining, but care should be taken not to offend anyone, and ensure that he performs his duties on behalf of the bridesmaids.

- The Best Man thanks the Bride and Groom for the gifts that they have just given out.
- He then compliments the rest of the wedding party, such as the Bridesmaids, Ushers, Page Boys, Flower Girls etc.
- He may wish to share some of the behind the scenes stories about wedding preparations, any amusing incidents or near missed disasters.
- Make sure you suggest that he includes the Bride, but don't embarrass her or raise a joke at her expense. Even if you don't think that she will mind, a lot of the guests will think it is improper.
- The traditional Best Man speech is about embarrassing the Groom. He should be funny without being offensive, and should not be nasty or risqué.
- It is ok for him to mention past relationships or the stag party, but tread carefully, if you have the slightest inclination that it might upset the Bride then suggest that they leave it out.
- Be kind about the Groom as well, he could mention how long they've been friends what he likes about him, and mention some good times that they have shared.
- Congratulate him on his wife, and how everyone hopes they will be happy together.
- Read any messages or telegrams from invited guests that have been unable to attend the wedding at the end of your speech.
- Conclude with a toast to the Bride and Groom.

Cutting the Cake

19

Most photographers will want to take a photograph of the couple cutting their cake. When they actually do cut their cake, this is an opportunity for all the guests to get involved and take photos too. Therefore, it is not the best time for the photographer to try to take a picture, as they will not be able to get the couple in the best position. Therefore, most couples will go into the reception room, with the photographer, prior to the reception starting (as guests enjoy their welcome drinks) and take a photograph of them pretending to cut the cake. Later on, in front of their guests they will formally cut the cake.

The actual timing of when the couple cut their cake can vary. It can be done either before the speeches, or after the speeches, or some couples choose to wait until the evening guests arrive.

Some couples choose to serve their cake as dessert or after dessert with the coffee. In which case, you may want to recommend that they cut the cake when everyone takes their seats for dinner, so that the catering staff will have enough time to serve it.

If the guests have eaten a generous meal, then you may wish to suggest that the cake isn't served with the coffee, purely because it's not eaten and gets wasted.

Courtesy of Danni Beach Photography www.dannibeachphotography.com

Wedding Planners Emergency Kit 20

You may have heard of an 'emergency kit'. This is literally just some supplies that hopefully will help you in most eventualities. Over time your emergency kit will grow, and you'll be amazed at how much 'stuff' you've accumulated.

The majority of items in your 'kit' will stay in your kit and you will use the same kit at every wedding, but may take additional items with you depending on the location and colour scheme of the wedding.

The best way to ensure you have everything you may need is to run through all the elements of the day that you know of, for instance, will the table plan be going on an easel, and have you seen the plan and the easel? Many venues' easel is a flip chart, so you may want to take something to cover the board. Or, you may know the colour is ivory and blue in which case take some ivory ribbon just in case.

As part of your preparation and planning you will have a list of the day's suppliers, you should include in your 'kit' a list of 'back up or alternative suppliers'.

In the space below, start thinking about some items you could start to collect for your 'emergency kit'

Activity

If you're nice to people, they'll help you out!! So for instance, florists usually have a back up of pins or wire that you can use.

Ideas For Your Wedding Planners Emergency Kit:

- Sellotape
- White ribbon
- Safety Pins
- Double sided sticky tape
- Plain name cards
- White plain card
- Scissors
- Sticky backed Velcro
- Cake dowling and pillars
- Matches
- Balloons
- Balloon hand pump
- Blu tack
- Pins
- White golf Umbrella
- Change for parking
- Camera
- Plasters
- Tea lights & Tea light holders
- Sewing kit
- Tissues
- Children's toys/colouring books & pencils
- Sun tan lotion
- Emergency contact information for suppliers
- Emergency wedding music

Throughout this book, there have been hints and tips on how to deal with, manage and create good working relationships with all suppliers.

In general you have to consider how you would appreciate to be treated. Someone suggesting that you don't know what you're doing, is likely to irritate you and wouldn't help you start off your working relationship together well.

Therefore it is suggested that you approach the initial conversation with an introduction and explanation of your role (for example assisting the Bride). Then ask to 'check' the information you have is correct against their records to ensure that you have your information and timetable right.

More often that not – this approach works, although everyone is different and some people just want to be difficult, and at those times you have to be assertive back and do not get bullied or swayed into performing in any manner other than that your client expects.

During the wedding day, it's advisable to get suppliers (bands, DJs, photographers, videographers) drinks. Food is more difficult – especially if it hasn't been pre-ordered. If there is a cash bar at the wedding, then have a chat with the couple prior to the day to ask them how, or if, they will be providing soft drinks.

Courtesy of Danni Beach Photography
www.dannibeachphotography.com

It is inevitable that at some point something will go wrong. The best prevention is to a) be aware of the common hiccups, but b) is to have thought about some mitigating actions should something happen. The best advice is to stay calm, reason with yourself the importance of the 'hiccup' such as a cake tier not being cooked….do you tell the bride or just cut another tier….

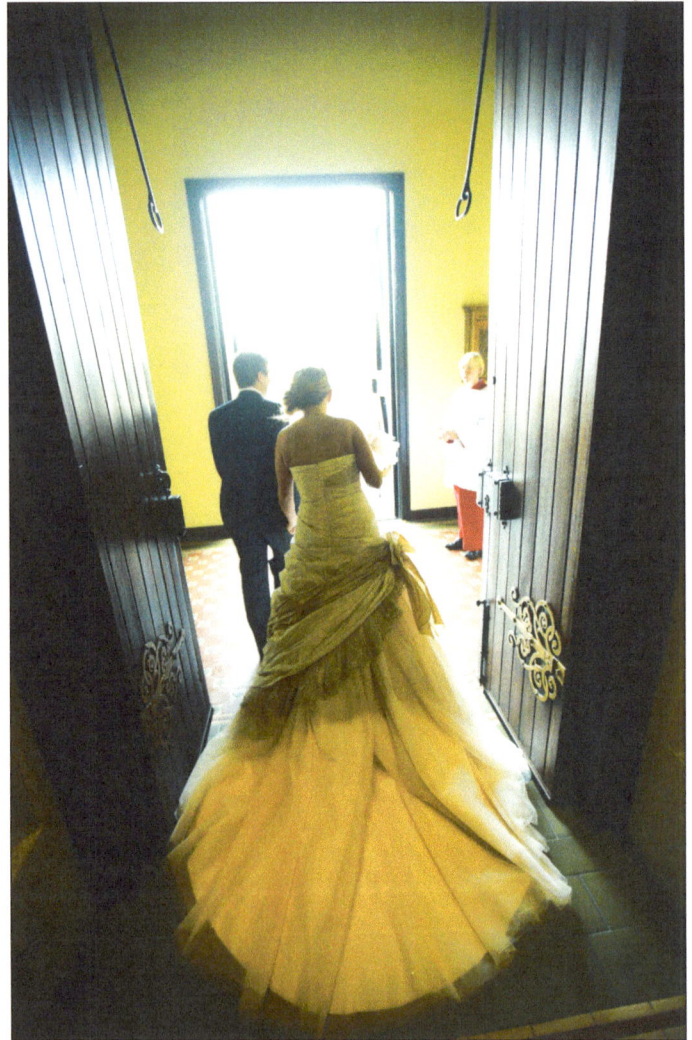

It is worth taking time prior to a wedding day and considering the most likely accidents/hiccups and what you would do in the scenario to solve it.

2.1 Building Your Experience

Getting started is the hardest thing, and before you launch yourself in headfirst, have a think about what you want to do and why. Maybe you just want to offer the 'on the day' service, or, you could work in a venue and expand your role so you take on the extra responsibilities as detailed herein, so that you offer your clients so much more than they get elsewhere.

It's worth thinking about doing a business plan which will help you decide on the approach you will take to build your experience, get clients and collect testimonials and a portfolio.

You may wish to launch and offer special incentives to get clients to choose you. That could be running competitions at Bridal Shows that you attend, or putting a special code in adverts that people can book to get a £50 discount.

Advertising, as already discussed requires a high investment, and in order to get a high brand awareness you will need to let people know that you have launched. If you are prepared to offer your services for no cost, you will need to be able to maintain this arrangement for the length of their planning.

Try to get experience shadowing wedding planners that are already established, and look for opportunities, in high season as a free pair of hands on a wedding day, or for freelance opportunities.

Understanding the roles of your suppliers is vital. By assisting them at weddings, or by working at a wedding venue on wedding days, you'll be able to use these experiences as examples when you are talking to couples. By using real examples you will be able to convince them of your knowledge and capability.

Most couples ask many questions about the ceremony. Try to get experience in Churches, or Civil Wedding venues where you can watch the ceremony and be able to offer advice on good hymns to choose or readings. What can go wrong (such as a fast processional or one that is too slow).

Each wedding planning company has a different approach when it comes to their portfolio and demonstrating their expertise.

The way you choose to do it needs to be right for you.

If you work at a venue, then try to take photographs with 'BEFORE' and 'AFTER' shots, to show how a room can be transformed. This will capture the Bride and Groom as they can then imagine their wedding in the room.

Some couples like to see testimonials from suppliers to say that you're good to work with! Suppliers will also be able to share their photographs with you of weddings which they have worked on.

Visit some suppliers and watch how they explain their services to you. Some will use a portfolio, others won't. This will help you decide whether it.s something you'll like to do.

Whilst most courses and wedding planners will tell you that you must have a portfolio – if your weddings aren't impressive enough (and don't have the WOW factor), or if you do 4 weddings in your first year, will you have a big enough or high quality portfolio that will win you business?

A testimonial is a very valuable tool in helping you get credibility and a good reputation. Pictures say a thousand words, so keep friendly with your photographer and try to get some good, impressive shots for your website or literature.

Finally, Good Luck in your career as a Wedding Planner.

Templates

Initial Consultation Template

Pre-Meeting Information:

Customer Name(s)	
Email:	
Phone Number:	
Address:	
Date of Enquiry:	
Date of Appointment:	
Time:	
Location:	

Details of Enquiry:

Items sent to Customer:

Wedding Day Information	
Proposed Wedding Date:	
Time of year/time of day:*If date not known.*	
Type of Wedding e.g. Church/Civil	
Ideas of Locations	
Overview of the wedding they want	
Estimated number of guests: Day/Evening/Children	
What services do they want from a wedding planner	
Budget	

Wedding Location	In here you would record what they are looking for and the most important aspects for them; or what they have already chosen/booked
For Ceremony	
For Reception	
For Evening Reception	
Any other ideas?	
Decoration:	
Room Decorations	
Theme ideas	
Table Decorations	
Transport	
To ceremony	
To reception	
Wedding Party cars	
Guest transportation	
Wedding Day Suppliers	
Hairdresser	
Make up artist	
Stationery	

Flowers	
Photographer	
Videographer	
Cake	
Toastmaster	

Entertainment	
Music at Ceremony	
Music at Welcome Drinks	
Music during Wedding Breakfast	
Music during Evening	
Other entertainment	

Catering	Details will vary whether catering in venue or separate supplier
Type of Meals Day/Evening	
Drink arrangements	

Accommodation	
Pre-Wedding Night	
Wedding Night	
Guests	

Initial Consultation – Crib Sheet - Template

You may find following a 'crib-sheet' helpful at your initial consultation meetings to ensure you cover everything you wish to say

Ask Bride about the wedding

If already chatted to a Bride about her wedding, does she have any update on her plans/ ideas since you last spoke?

Overview of your company:

How long have you been established?

What is your experience (you may want to mention small & large weddings you have been involved in)

The service you provide

Where you have worked

Offer an out of hours service - contactable after work and at weekends & constant support via email

Why you recommend having a consultation

Able to provide a clear understanding of the role and involvement Bride would like you to have with her wedding, you will be able to provide her with an estimated quote for your services – that suit her requirements.

Emphasise the need to feel completely comfortable with your co-ordinator and trust that they will listen to your wishes and ideas

So you can see 'your company' in person and get a feel for our passion and work ethic towards you wedding

Benefit in having a wedding planner

Able to negotiate discounts and special rates with suppliers - which are not available to Brides themselves.

Cost effective - we will keep you to your budget and in some cases help your wedding day to come in under budget!!

Calm and quick thinking on the day – not as emotionally involved, so can solve any hiccups logically and without fuss.

You are a wedding expert – have worked on many weddings, all with different requirements and budgets and ethnicities or cultures (example: Afro Caribbean, Sikh, Jewish, French, Turkish).

You service can be tailored to suit their needs and requirements regardless of whether the event is large or small.

Remove the burden of the mass of details, and see that each segment of your wedding is properly planned and implemented.

Can provide you with worksheets, planning calendars, check lists and fact sheets which contain ideas and suggestions.

Provide some testimonials if required

Describe and explain your services

Explain how you can help at any stage, whether just 'on the day' or create a package to suit your needs

Ask about the budget/amount in mind to pay for service

Discuss what you can do within that budget

Closing statement

Any questions

Would they be interested in your service, and you provide any references, further information etc.

Wedding Day Co-ordination Pre-Meeting Template

(For use for 'on the day" services)

Name	
Wedding Date	
Budget	
Number of Guests	
Ceremony	
Breakfast	
Evening	

Overview of day (i.e. theme etc.)

Type of Ceremony	Civil / Religious
	DETAILS
Time	
Location	

Reception	
Location	

Arrangements made:	
Entertainment Wedding	
Entertainment Post Wedding	
Entertainment Evening	
Ceremony Decorations Order of Services Flowers Confetti	
Venue & Reception Decoration Table decorations Stationery Chair Covers	
Transport (to Church From Church)	
Photography	
Videography	

Floristry	
Dress	
Suit Hire	
MC -	
Theme	
Timetable concerns:	
Payments to be made:	Record in here any payments which need to be made on the wedding day to suppliers.

Proposal of Services – Example Template

Client Ref: xxxx   Date xx/xx/xx

Dear Bride and Groom,

Thank you again for sparing some time to meet with me, and many thanks for allowing me the opportunity to provide a quote for my services, to assist you with your wedding plans. I have detailed below a list of the services that I will be able to provide you for your wedding day based on the requirements I understood from our meeting.

Details of Service –

Sourcing and Managing the following suppliers: - **Gospel Choir, transport, marquee, lighting, bar and all interior and exterior décor, toilets, caterers, florist, topiary, fireworks, security, photographer, ice sculpture, cake, stationery, favours, confetti/petals, candles and lanterns, additional entertainment for the day – such as Band and DJ.** These will be sourced in order of priority and you will be offered a choice of suppliers where appropriate, to allow you to choose the one you are happiest with.

Assistance with budget management: - I will work with you to create an estimated budget and to allocate the budget against the key items of the wedding day. I will create a payment schedule so you know what payments are due and when. I will endeavour to keep you within your desired budget and I can advise on an ideal amount to spend on each supplier, but ultimately it will be your decision as to how much you would like to spend on each supplier and what level of service you require. You would receive copies of all quotes and invoices provided.

Help and Advice on the theme of the day: - To ensure the day has a coherent feel and looks the way you want, I will create a mood board; putting together ideas we discuss to clarify your vision for your day and give it the 'wow' factor. This is great to show suppliers.

Accommodation for guests: - I can arrange to block reserve rooms at suitable hotels for your guests. Guests would be responsible for booking their own accommodation.

Information sheet for guests: - I will create, with the stationer, an essential information guide for your guests including places to stay, directions, timelines etc.

Meetings: - I will attend all supplier meetings, including any that required bride or groom's presence (e.g. florist, marquee, etc.). Plus up to six additional meetings which can be used to discuss any concerns or worries and help us to move the plans forward. Good communication will be essential to plan your day successfully.

Week of the wedding attendance- I will oversee the erection of the marquee, delivery of all the necessary items and liaise closely with all the suppliers. I will also attend the church rehearsal so everyone knows what he or she should be doing and where they should be standing etc.

I will stay over locally the night before the wedding to ensure I could be on site 'bright and early' on the day of the wedding, and can deal with any issues as they arise.

Preparation for and attendance on the day including: Assisting with the exact layout of the marquee, double checking all bookings and providing suppliers with their final instructions, payments etc. I will prepare a very detailed time line for the day so suppliers and yourselves would know what was happening and when, as well as devising my 'on the day' task list. On the day itself I would attend from the time agreed and detailed in the timeline to ensure your day runs smoothly and as planned, including attendance at the Church to sooth those last minute nerves, I will also have a colleague working with me so we can be in two places at once! I will be working in the background dealing with any issues and liaising closely with all suppliers. I will leave once all major events had occurred i.e. fireworks finale - leaving you to enjoy the party!

Day after attendance- After spending a second night locally I will attend the following morning to oversee any tidy up that was required before the furniture company and marquee company arrive to take away their equipment. Ensuring all flowers were collected and moved to your home, and the florist is able to collect any vases or display equipment that has been hired.

Administration and Advice – I will deal with all administration that is required for your wedding. Letters or calls from suppliers will not bother you, as everything would be directed to me. However I will provide you with copies of contracts (prior to agreement), invoices etc. I will be available to advise and guide you on all aspects of your day throughout the year either via email, phone or face-to-face meetings (as detailed above).

Total price £xx

Other notes:

This quote is valid for x days

This price also includes cost of overnight accommodation on two nights, the assistance of a second planner on the wedding day, postage, phone calls (up to 9pm - 7 days a week), unlimited emails, mileage for the wedding day and stated meeting.

I would require a meal and unlimited soft drinks to be provided for my colleague and myself on the day of the wedding and the following day. This does not need to be the same as the guests' menu.

Payment terms:

Supplier Recommendations Template

(you can use this template for items such as table cameras, name cards, table favours)

Company Name	Website	Cost per item	Comments

Recommendations:

You may want to write in here your own recommendations taking into account:

- companies that you have used before
- those which offer you a trade discount
- which companies offer a selection of the items you need, so that the cost of delivery combining delivery, may make them more attractive overall, but may seem more expensive on an individual basis
- consideration for delivery times
- consideration for any duty and tax charges for items being delivered from abroad.

Supplier Comparison Template

(an example below is with the catering costs)

	Supplier 1	Supplier 2	Supplier 3
Canapés			
Welcome drink			
3 glasses wine with meal			
3 course meal			
Evening buffet			
Champagne toasts			
Room Rate per night			

Supplier Comparison Template

(an example below is with a one type of supplier such as DJ/Chair Covers)

Supplier 1 - NAME

Website:

Overview:
include here experience in the industry and their preferred style, whether you have worked with them before. Key terms in the contract.

Cost:
Be clear to show actual cost for service/product (does it include VAT)
Mileage/Travel costs
Refreshments required/Accommodation required

Supplier 2 - NAME

Website:

Overview:
include here experience in the industry and their preferred style, whether you have worked with them before. Key terms in the contract.

Cost:
Be clear to show actual cost for service/product (does it include VAT)
Mileage/Travel costs
Refreshments required/Accommodation required

Supplier 3 - NAME

Website:

Overview:
include here experience in the industry and their preferred style, whether you have worked with them before. Key terms in the contract.

Cost:
Be clear to show actual cost for service/product (does it include VAT)
Mileage/Travel costs
Refreshments required/Accommodation required

RECOMMENDATIONS:
detail here, your views on the suppliers and which you recommend. Do also let the couple now, when you need a decision by.

Example Press Release Template

Date
FOR IMMEDIATE RELEASE:

Contact:
Contact Person
Company Name
Telephone Number
Fax Number
Email Address
Web site address

Headline
Town, County, Date — Opening Paragraph (should contain: who, what, when, where, why):

Remainder of body text - Should include any relevant information to your products or services. Include benefits, why your service is unique. Also include quotes from staff members, industry experts or satisfied customers.
If there is more than 1 page use:

-more-

(The top of the next page):
Abbreviated headline (page 2)
Remainder of text.

(Restate Contact information after your last paragraph):
For additional information, contact: (all Contact information)

Summarise service specifications one last time
Company History (try to do this in one short paragraph)

#
(indicates Press Release is finished)

Feedback Form Template

Wedding Planning Services Comments Form

Bride & Groom:

Wedding date:

Your Wedding Coordinator/ Planner:

Thank you for choosing 'COMPANY NAME', could you tell us where you learnt about us, and what made you choose our services?

Do you feel that the service you received from 'COMPANY NAME' was value for money?

Can you think of a situation when 'COMPANY NAME' exceeded your expectations and/or went beyond the call of duty? What did we do? Why was it so helpful?

'COMPANY NAME' is driven towards providing the best service we possibly can, so for the benefit of future brides, was there anything we could have done differently or improved on? Or perhaps there was a service we didn't provide that would have been useful?

We like to hold a portfolio of photographs of weddings that we have had the privilege of being part of. Are you happy for us to include your wedding in this portfolio? You are welcome to review the images that we select for our portfolio.

Are there any other comments that you would like to make?

Please note that we like to use customers' comments as part of our business literature. Please advise if you would not like us to quote anything that you have written.

Lightning Source UK Ltd.
Milton Keynes UK
UKHW051438020619
343704UK00004B/38/P